Out of Fear
into
Love

Praise

High praise indeed for *Out Of Fear, Into Love*. Marléne has created an outstanding book here that really connects and draws the reader in without them feeling overwhelmed in the process.

What I so love about this book is Marléne explains things in a way that makes you think: 'Oh yes, that happened to me, I can relate to that.' For me it was the story of the child putting his hand up at school to answer a question and when the teacher asked him, he got it wrong, all the other children laughed. A simple event like that can have a huge impact on a child who grows up with a fear of speaking up, and a self-limiting belief about being heard in the world.

Within the pages you are about to enjoy reading you will come to understand, through well written true-life events how self-limiting beliefs can disrupt ones' joy of living and make life a struggle, when it clearly does not need, or is not meant to be. Marléne offers tools and exercises to reframe our blocks so that life will work for you more easily. This book has visual aids which helps those that work with a more visual mind, as opposed to an analytical one. I know from my own journey that learning to love oneself is very important, and is the key to living life to your fullest potential, so anything that helps and guides a person to that point of self-love and self-acceptance, is in my view, a blessing.

I hope you enjoy reading this book as much as I did, and I wish you well on your journey of life and self-discovery. Big thanks and much love to Marléne for creating such a marvellous book.

James Gardner, author of *How To Heal From Trauma and PTSD: Your Ultimate Guide To Becoming The Person You want To Be*

One of the biggest challenges that we all face in life is an often imperceptible fear, which becomes a driving force behind everything that we do. In *Out of Fear, Into Love*, Marléne Shaw has made a unique contribution to helping us recognize when we are operating from this place of fear. She has also presented us with a series of strategies that help us to effectively move beyond it. This book has a perfect balance of personal story, unique concepts, case studies, tools and practices. It enables the reader to not only move beyond any fear they are feeling, but to also move towards experiencing more love in their life. It's a highly practical manual that the reader will pick up time and time again, and it will help them to befriend their emotions and expand their self-love as a result.

Sasha Allenby, co-author of *Matrix Reimprinting Using EFT*, author of *Write an Evolutionary Self-Help Book*

Even after all the self-development work I've done, reading this book had me in tears. Of joy, relief, connectedness and love. Marléne's book gently takes us from understanding how we get stuck in our struggles, to practical tips, exercises and strategies we can use to move out of strife and into a loving space to create our lives anew.

This book is a game changer. If you've ever struggled with having too much on your plate and feeling resentful about it, or feeling envious that others' lives appear so much easier than yours, then this book is for you. It will help you if you find it hard to ask for help, yet limp along by yourself, exhausted and overwhelmed. It will help you if you often have the feeling that you need to prove yourself and find yourself wanting to please people at your own expense. *Out of Fear, Into Love* offers simple, enjoyable tools of change to go from a life of struggle to self-love and ease. It's beautifully written, radiating what it speaks of: We can never be separated from love. We may just need some help to remember that love is what we ARE. Marléne's book needs to be in every home and library!

Liesel Teversham, Author of *No Problem. The Upside of Saying No*

www.savvyselfgrowth.com

Marléne Rose Shaw has skilfully put into writing the process she has used to assist her therapy clients to transform their limiting beliefs. *Out of Fear, Into Love* is a thoughtful and effective guidebook. The heart of the book describes four common limiting beliefs about struggle, and Marléne offers both clear case studies that are easy to relate with and practical exercises to help you make real shifts. Lack of self-love and lack of self-care are at the root of many emotional blocks, and I am inspired by how well this book addresses what self-love is and how to recover it. This is a book to DO, not just skim. The Transformation Process is aptly named, and I'm confident that if you work through it from start to finish you'll be happy with the results.

Jack Stephens, Author of *Soul Self: How to Tame Your Mind, Uncover Your Blueprint, and Live Your Soul Purpose*

Marlene has created a lovely, reassuring book drawing on her many years of experience as a therapist. Her gentle, understanding approach immediately puts you at your ease, as she takes you on a journey that is easy for us all to relate to. With the help of case studies of clients, Marlene clearly explains the reasons why so many of us find life a struggle. She takes us by the hand and enables us to acknowledge and thank our inner child for striving to keep us safe for so many years. Her step by step transformation process guides us to a kinder and more resourceful way of living. If you ever question whether there is more to life than struggle, this book is for you!

Sue Williams, Lead author of *Believe You Can Face Your Fears and Confidently Claim the Life You Desire*

If life has always been a struggle, *Out of Fear, Into Love* is the book for you. It offers a range of transformational tools and techniques to release the emotional blocks that keep you stuck in a life of survival. After reading this wonderful book of wisdom you'll find yourself falling in love with life and thriving. Moving out of fear and into love is a journey you won't regret taking—you'll only wish you did it sooner.

Wendy Fry, Author of *Find YOU, Find LOVE: Get to the heart of love and relationships using EFT*

Out of Fear
into
Love

*Life Doesn't Have
to Be a Struggle*

By

Marléne Rose Shaw

Published by Power of Love Books

POWER OF LOVE
BOOKS

ISBN: 978-0-9935419-0-2

Editor: Lois Rose

Illustrator: Jamie Shaw

Publishing services provided by:

 **Archangel Ink**

For Jamie
With Love

Acknowledgements

Special Gratitude to:

Lois Rose: the most patient of editors

Sasha Allenby: my inspiration and teacher

Gary Craig: for bringing EFT into the world

Karl Dawson: for teaching me EFT

Cathy Davey: for giving me confidence

Wendy Fry: who encouraged me and led the way

Kavin Hoo: whose inspiring music shone a light on the path

Jamie Shaw: for his outstanding artwork

Contents

The Transformation Process: Part Three: Into Love.... 115

List of Practices and Worksheets

How to Get the Very Best from this Book

The Journey

When clients come to me for therapy, I guide them through a journey of transformation. It's a journey that leaves struggle behind and takes them into freedom and happiness, and it follows a particular route, not always linear but with a clearly established beginning, middle, and end. I've written this book very much in-line with that journey so that you, the reader, can travel the same path as my clients.

As we embark on any journey, it's always helpful to have some idea of our destination—in this case, some vision of what a new and happier life is going to look like. With this in mind, I'll start by sharing what I've learnt from many years as a therapist about what makes people truly happy.

Next, I'll go on to look at what stops us from achieving that happiness. I'll explore how approaching life from a perspective of fear and struggle affects the different parts of our lives and how we first came to view life in these unhelpful ways.

Most importantly, I'll be sharing with you the two main reasons why people often find it so hard to shift that perspective, and what can be done to remove those blocks to more easily make positive changes and begin to live a happy, struggle-free life.

I'll introduce you to The Transformation Process, a specific method for emotional healing, developed through my work over thousands of client sessions. The Transformation Process has a particular order. In each part, you'll find helpful techniques and practices which, whilst being very useful on their own, lay the groundwork for the next part. To get the very best from this book then, I recommend that you work through it from the beginning, covering each part of the process in the order presented.

Your Special Notebook

I often give my clients a notebook to use during their therapeutic journey; it's useful for homework exercises and for writing down relevant thoughts and memories in between sessions. I suggest that you, too, provide yourself with a notebook to jot down your own relevant thoughts and memories as they come up for you.

In some chapters I'll be sharing examples from case studies which you may well resonate with from your own experiences — your notebook can come in handy then too, for jotting down your thoughts and memories as they pop into your mind. It's often the case that thoughts, realisations, and memories come to us at random times: as we're washing up, walking the dog, on a train etc., so it's a great idea to have your notebook with you at these times, too.

How you organise your notebook is entirely up to you; some people like to scribble down notes in the order they come to mind, other people like to organise their notes in to categories: choose what suits you, but make sure you treat your notebook as an integral part of your journey through this book.

I recommend you use an attractive new notebook specifically for this purpose; it adds a sense of specialness for you, and it inspires you and reminds you of your worthiness in taking this wonderful step into your new and happier life.

Exercises

As you've probably seen, I've included a handy index of the practices and worksheets at the beginning of this book. These, plus the written examples in the book, can be downloaded from the website at www.outoffearintolove.com

You'll also find the guided mp3 meditation *Trust* for Chapter Thirteen: *Into Love: The Power in Trust*, available to download.

I've also added some bonus materials on the website.

Icons

Whenever a download is available, you will see the following icon:

You will also see two other icons:

Reminder to make a note:

Point of Interest:

Resources

'Resources' also includes a list of references and further information for you, such as other books on the topics covered and relevant websites.

Contact Information

I've also included my contact information if you would like to book one-to-one sessions with me via Skype or at my private practice.

Much as it can be uncomfortable to reach this point of discontent, there *is* a positive side to it. It's the beginning of self-awareness, and self-awareness is the seed of personal transformation.

Introduction

For some people it's dramatic. Something comes along, seemingly out of the blue, and hits them square between the eyes — an experience which is so intense they know immediately that something has to change. For others, it's more of a quiet knowing that builds up over time.

That's how it was for me — quiet.

It had been hovering in the back of my mind for a while. Then one day, it just softly clicked into place, as though a piece of a puzzle had found its rightful place in my conscious awareness. It was the thought:

'I don't have to struggle anymore.'

Up until that point, struggling had been a natural way of life for me.

As far back as I could remember, there had been some issue to deal with — some problem to overcome or hardship to endure. In every area of my life I spent a lot of time and energy trying to please people, prove myself, and earn acceptance: my own, and others'. It was a pretty exhausting way to live.

I had a habit of taking on too much responsibility for other people's problems, yet for myself I never asked for help. In fact, I prided myself on doing things all by myself. I fought hard to gain qualifications and a career, all the while as a single parent. There was nothing I liked better than to put on my superhero cape and show the world just how strong and capable I was.

It seems strange to me now that for all those years I truly believed this was how my life was supposed to be! I always assumed other people had an easier life because they were just lucky, and so I accepted my own life as not being so lucky and took on board whatever turned up for me. But this came with some resentment at my 'lot in life,' and particularly when I compared myself to those other, luckier, people.

Somewhere along the line, the seeds of discontent took root and I began to think about those happy people and question – what was it about their lives that was so different to mine? Sure, they had better relationships, more money, more rewarding work, but how were they, as people, actually different to me?

And because I'd asked this question, the universe gently answered me with a dawning realisation. I began to recognise that those happy people *expected* life to be good, they expected to have better relationships, they expected to have more money and rewarding work, and they were confident that this was how life was going to be for them, without question.

That was the difference!

I'd always expected that life was going to be a struggle; that I had to put up with problems, earn and please and prove my way into happiness. It was a revelation to me. It was the dawn of my new life.

And although I wasn't aware of it at the time, looking back now, I can clearly see that I was also often drawn towards struggle-type situations. They seemed familiar to me. I even created new struggles to deal with where before there had been none. Several of my relationships had been, to some degree, insecure and stressful. I was attracted to partners and friends who had problems of their own. I also had a tendency to push away those emotionally healthier people who wanted to offer me genuine care and support.

Of course, I wasn't to blame for this. No more than anyone is to be blamed for the struggles they experience – we just learn these unhelpful 'ways of being' early on in life, and we carry on like this until we get so fed up with being unhappy that we start to wonder if life could possibly be different. Much as it can be uncomfortable to reach this point of discontent, there *is* a positive side to it. It's the beginning of self-awareness, and self-awareness is the seed of personal transformation.

But, you know, my experience of life as a struggle in those days isn't an uncommon phenomenon. When people come into therapy they very often tell me they're fed up of battling with problems that keep cropping up in their lives. People don't come into therapy because they *have* a problem. They come into therapy because they're *stuck* in a problem — either it won't go away, or it does go for a while, but then re-presents itself further down the line. It may be that in their work they feel undervalued and pressurised. Or in their relationships they have the same old quarrels, and they feel taken for granted and disrespected. Physically they may be stressed and have symptoms that never quite clear up. Whatever the issue happens to be, they always feel caught up in unhappy emotions, such as resentment, guilt, anger, or anxiety.

And when we look just a little further, it's often the case that these same issues have been coming up regardless of where they live, or work, or the people they spend time with — and often these same issues have spanned decades of their lives.

One thing I never hear from a new client is:

> **'Hey, I have this problem and I just want to share with you that I'm working through it, I'm growing wiser and I'm creating a life I love!'**

Instead they say:

> **'I've got this problem and I don't know what to do… I keep coming back round to this same situation… I don't know how to change it… Is it me that's making this happen?'**

Over the years I've noticed that while people may bring different problems into therapy, there's a common theme that seems to underpin their discontent. That theme is the firm belief that the path to happiness can only be found through struggling in some way: earning validation, putting up with hardships, proving, and pleasing, and striving alone. I've seen this pattern of **'First I have to struggle, and then I get to be happy'** present itself in my clients again and again. I've seen it in all ages and I've seen it in all walks of life.

Taking this approach to life never really brings happiness. It makes it impossible to feel content for very long because, when we put so much pressure on ourselves, we simply perpetuate our problems rather solving them. In perpetuating those problems, we reinforce the mistaken idea that **'life's a struggle,'** and so it goes on in a never-ending cycle. That's why we so often come back to the same old problems, no matter where we go or what we do.

Over time, I've developed The Transformation Process: a method that has enabled me to help many, many people let go of struggle and change their lives for the better to find real and lasting happiness. Now, I want to reach more people, and that's why I've written this book.

Just like the people I've helped over the years, it's very likely that you're here with me at the start of this journey because the time is right for you. You're ready to make some changes and to step into a wonderful, new, struggle-free life of lasting happiness; I'm so excited for you because I know that if you read through this book and follow the techniques and worksheets, your whole life is going to change forever.

So let's begin!

Most children see life from this perspective of 'Wow!' They delight in everything; they seem to know that they're part of something much greater than themselves — a powerful force which is always supporting them.

Chapter One
The Universal Elements of Happiness

'The universe supports life; it flows freely to all and is endlessly abundant.'
Dr Wayne W. Dyer

Have you ever asked a small child, 'Where do you live?' and they've told you their address, the country they live in, and then they've continued on to a triumphant:

'Planet Earth... The Galaxy... The Universe!'

Most children see life from this perspective of 'Wow!' They delight in everything and they seem to know that they're part of something much greater than themselves — a powerful force which is always supporting them. And life is good.

Small children are intrigued by every little thing; they just *have* to explore their world. They're filled with awe and wonder at each new discovery: a leaf, a spider's web, a fluffy cloud — it's as if they're simply in love with life itself.

There was very likely a time when you were the same; perhaps you can look back now and still recall a few memories of that time? Maybe you thrilled at splashing in puddles, or you marvelled at rainbows that seemed to hover like magic in the sky, just for you?

A Magical Story

And because children start out from a place of 'This is all wonderful!' so it *is* all wonderful for them. They seem to know without question that life is a special gift and that they can be masters of their own destiny.

'When I grow up, I want to be a train driver, a builder, a film star,' they say as they dream their dreams and come up with new and different versions of how the story of their life is going to be. And of course it's always going to be a magical story — there's no expectation that life could be otherwise!

Every one of us has our own special story. Even though there are seven billion of us on our beautiful planet Earth, each of us is unique. Our stories are the dreams we dream and the adventures we have. They are our disappointments and our successes and all that happens in between. Our stories create the chapters of our lives, and each one is different to the last, as we learn and grow and become inspired by new dreams and different possibilities.

And as we move through life, we attach 'happiness value' to different things: our possessions, our achievements, our goals, our relationships — and these attachments are as changeable as we ourselves are. Maybe you're aware that what once made you happy holds much less importance now, and what once seemed of little value to you is much more appreciated?

But much as these things change over time, I've come to recognise that there are three key elements that create a type of happiness that is lasting. It's a type of happiness that is independent of what we've got, or who we're with, or what we're doing, or even the stage of life we're at. These three essential elements of happiness are metaphysical in nature; they are ways of being that are part of the very fabric of our universe. As children we lived by these ways quite naturally; they were what thrilled us, and inspired us, and put the 'Wow!' into our lives. So what are these essential ways?

» We Desire to Create

» We Aspire to Connect

» We Seek to Evolve

When these are part of our experience of life we can't help but be happy because we're tuned in with life itself. Here's a closer look at them.

We Desire to Create

I'll always remember one day when my son was about eighteen months old. I had left him for his usual afternoon nap, and when I went to wake him he was sitting in his cot-bed with all his teddy bears lined up along the side. He was pointing to each of them in turn and chattering away, completely absorbed in some sort of 'group meeting.' It was the first time I saw him fully engaged in imaginary play; he was creating his own little world with all the characters playing different roles — it was enchanting to watch him and that memory still brings a smile to me now, many years later.

Whenever we're in a state of creativity, there's magic happening because we're being the master of our own destiny; we're deliberately making life happen just as we wish it to be. This is why small children love to play so much. They're little originators, testing out their creating skills, as they summon up imaginary friends or lose themselves in a world of magic and games.

And as adults we continue creating the story of our life by the choices we make. We choose our studies and our work, we form relationships, make a home, perhaps become a parent. We travel and explore and plan and dream of our future ... oh, we so love to dream! When nothing's happening in our lives we get bored, and so we seek out new adventures and re-organise parts of our life to create new experiences that will inspire us and make life interesting again. That's what creating our story really means — taking an aspect of our life and reshaping it into something new, something that takes us forward.

This is what our universe is always doing — shaping and reshaping, and creating anew — and we live out our lives in parallel with the universe, each of us tuning in with our creative energy to make our own story happen within the grander story of life itself.

When we're in tune with our creative energy, we're allowing the energy that creates all life to help us create our own life just as we wish it to be. Everything — our relationships, our work, our confidence — is easier and all of it becomes a story that is fun and inspiring and fulfilling.

We don't get stuck in problems. When challenges pop up, our creativity does the work for us; it gives us moments of inspiration and clarity by highlighting resourceful solutions.

Have you had one of those 'aha' moments when a solution to a problem seems to pop up out of nowhere as if by magic? That's the creative energy of the universe giving you a helping hand. It makes sense then that being tuned in with our creativity is always going to make us happier because it helps us reach our full potential.

We Aspire to Connect

Two adults sitting next to each other on a train may possibly strike up a conversation, but more often than not they don't. They sit in silence, each in their own world, maybe absorbed in their problems, or perhaps shy and unsure how to open up a dialogue.

Two children sitting next to each other on a train will very often start chattering away; eager and interested in what they have to share with each other in this exciting world. They have no need to analyse the situation — they don't stop to consider whether it's OK to speak to each other, they just do it! The adults look on fondly, their hearts warmed by this display of kinship; they possibly smile at each other with a knowing look, an inherent understanding that the magic of connectedness is taking place before them.

Life *is* connectedness. It's a constant state of interaction.

We each exist within a body, which is sustained by intricate co-operating systems. We live in communities where we connect through mutual support and sharing our skills so that we can sustain our lives. And, in turn, our communities are part of the natural world where no part of life can act completely independently of another; our oceans, land, atmosphere and climate all exist as one interconnected system — a continuous exchange of dynamic energy. Connectedness, then, is a fundamental state of being; it's a magical force that organises and supports life. When we experience it, we feel good and life is easier. When we don't experience it, we feel bad and life is a struggle.

One of the most obvious ways we experience connectedness is through our relationships. And the most important of these is the relationship we have with our own self. If we're cut off from our self because we judge and criticise our self, it's harder to manage challenging situations in life. We feel vulnerable and unworthy, so we tend to look outwardly to others to validate us as being good enough. And those relationships with others, then, become hard work too.

When we find ways to have a loving relationship with ourselves, that's tuning in to the energy of connectedness; it brings us healthier relationships with others — in kinship, intimacy, and togetherness. All this brings us support and wellbeing so that we can move forward and feel inspired and happier.

We Seek to Evolve

When we're in tune with our creative energy and we have the magical power of connection in our lives, we can much more easily grow and evolve into our wisdom. And wisdom is what it's all about! We're wisdom seekers at our very core; we feel happy and inspired when we're learning something about ourselves, and life. We just love figuring things out; we're hardwired to seek out expansion because we're part of a universe that's doing the very same.

People tend to associate the word 'wisdom' with older people, but our quest to know, and to grow, starts at the very beginning. Little children are so eager to explore and discover their world; they don't worry about getting it right, they just get curious!

And we carry on wanting to explore life and learn as we grow into adulthood. The thought of standing still is displeasing to us. That's why it feels so bad when we keep coming up against the same old problems in life, because we feel we haven't learnt anything. It's that stuck-ness that's so uncomfortable.

It's very often the interactions we have with each other that provide the greatest opportunity to learn and grow. Because we're all different, with our own ideas, our own dreams and desires, it's inevitable that we'll 'bump up' against each other sometimes. And that's a great opportunity to make sense of our differences and mature a little more. The people in our lives are there to play different roles, like characters in our story. Each of them is there in their own way to help us learn something, and to remember to love ourselves. It could be the friend taking us for granted, who's gently nudging us to value our worth. It could be the demanding colleague reminding us to be kinder and more accepting of our self. It could be the person who teaches us about forgiveness.

When we recognise each other – as teacher to guide us, and students to learn from us – we can start to view life as one big school of wisdom. Each time we come up against a challenging person, or a situation, instead of getting angry and resentful, we can step back and ask ourselves:

'What can I learn from this?'

And that's when the excitement happens, because we move a little further forward in our expansion.

As I've helped people make changes, it's become apparent to me that, alongside our everyday opportunities to expand our lives, we each have some bigger steps to take on our journey into wisdom. These are very personal to us; they may be problems in our relationships or achieving our goals, or they may be issues with confidence, or work, or lifestyle. These are the challenges that we have yet to learn from; they're the bigger wisdom lessons which wait patiently for us to catch up with them. They wait until we become so fed up with them showing up that our innate need to evolve nudges us to resolve them.

But whether we're becoming just a tiny bit wiser each day, or making big personal changes, life is a constant calling towards transformation. And as long as we're moving forward, we're happy. It's when we recognise this and accept that life is an ongoing journey into wisdom that we can be at our happiest.

The Beginning of Struggle

As we've seen, when we were children, these three elements were a natural part of our lives; we lived in harmony with our universe then, and we trusted that we were supported and loved, and all was well.

But somewhere along the line, often quite early in life, many of us lose that trust. This is the beginning of struggle. As we grow older, rather than living in harmony with our universe, we begin to feel disconnected and alone. Fear creeps in and steals our confidence; it takes away our belief that we're good enough, and it places blocks in the flow of our creativity. Life becomes less about ease and joy, and more about striving and struggle.

By the time we become adults, we assume that the ease of our long-ago childhood can only now come in glimpses: brief moments of inspiration, random times of closeness with others, occasional satisfaction through the achievement of something meaningful. It becomes the norm to think that these experiences are just down to luck because we no longer remember that we can be the creators of our own destinies.

The question is what happened? How did we forget? Why did life become such a struggle?

Because we keep filtering the world through the same lens, we keep being drawn to the same, familiar types of people and situations. Sometimes that's a good thing. Sometimes it's not such a good thing.

Chapter Two
Why is My Life Such a Struggle?

'We all throw rocks before us. One thing I've learned with certainty is that it's very hard to dance on rocks.'

Susan Jeffers

Have you noticed how some people seem to breeze through life with very few cares or worries? They appear to have it all: a great relationship, fulfilling work, a happy family, respect, and love. They're always having fun new experiences and they're full of confidence. How is it that they have such an easy life? Is it that they simply have good luck? They certainly seem to be tuned in to happiness and all flows well for them. For many others, however ... well, life's a struggle.

To struggle means finding something arduous or hard to achieve. We can struggle in a practical sense, as with a physical task, or grasping some complicated new skill — those things can be difficult sometimes. But then there's another type of struggle, a psychological and emotional way of *struggling with life itself.* This happens because we think that we have to be constantly overcoming some problem: keeping other people happy, proving ourselves, or being strong in the face of difficulties. It's as though we think that if we're not stressed in some way, then we're not really doing life properly! One part of us knows that life really could be a whole lot easier than we're making it for ourselves; the other part just can't seem to get out of the driving seat because we fear that if we're not in control life will fall apart. This is the phenomenon of struggle. It's very common and it can make itself known in every part of our lives. It shows up in our difficult relationships, and in the problems that come up at work. It shows up in our inability to achieve our dreams, and in our stress, and through our lack of self-confidence.

Am I Creating My Life, or Struggling to Survive it?

If your life seems to be one long road of problems and difficult relationships, a powerful question you can ask yourself is:

'Am I purposefully creating my own life, or am I simply struggling to survive it?'

There's a big difference between struggling to manage life's troubles, and being creators of our own destiny. When we struggle we're so focused on how *hard* everything is and how *alone* we are with it all; we cut ourselves off from support and make no room for inspiration or personal growth. When we let go of struggle—that's precisely when we start to 'live life on purpose' by choosing how we want things to be, rather than battling to overcome what life keeps handing us.

Somewhere in the Distance

But struggling is a deceptive way of living because it gives us the impression that by coping it means that we're in control of our lives. I sometimes think of struggling as approaching life like an obstacle course. Each obstacle represents a situation in which we have to prove ourselves as good enough, strong enough, worthy, likeable—loveable. We have this idea that happiness is just ahead, somewhere in the distance. We think that if we can just overcome the current obstacle due to a problematic person, or a difficult situation, *then* we'll reach our happiness. We often dream of the future when life will finally work out for us and we'll have a clear path in front of us. However, we never seem to quite get there because every time we manage to overcome one obstacle, another pops up in the form of another problematic person or difficult situation. And there always *will* be another obstacle to overcome because those struggles are not really about the troublesome people in our lives, or the challenging situations—they're really all about how we *approach* those relationships and those situations. Those struggles are all about how we look at life.

The Good News

There are far more of us who approach life from the perspective of struggle than not. It's little wonder that we may look at the minority of people who actually *are* truly happy and wonder:

'How is it that they come to have such an easy life when I don't?'

We may even view them with some resentment. However, the good news is we can be thankful to them, because they're a great reminder to us that life can indeed be happy and easy. And we can look at them and ask, 'What is it about the way they approach their lives that makes them so happy? What can I learn from them?'

We Each Filter the World through Our Own Personal Lens

I've always liked the insightful words of author Anaïs Nin who said:

'We don't see things as they are. We see things as we are.'

Life is a game of interpretation. We're constantly receiving information in the form of what people say, and do, and what we observe in the world. And we filter that information through our own individual lens. Our lens is made up of all the beliefs and ideas we've formed since childhood. It impacts on how we feel, how we think and behave, and all the choices and decisions we make in life. Many of our experiences therefore are based on the meaning we assign to a situation. And of course, if we're not fully aware of the lens through which we're peering, we'll go on having very similar experiences throughout our whole life.

We Get Drawn into What's Familiar

And because we keep filtering the world through the same lens, we keep being drawn to the same, familiar, types of people and situations. Sometimes that's a good thing. Sometimes it's not such a good thing.

Those happier people I mentioned tend to look at life through a lens that tells them: **Life is easy, I can do this, I'm worth it, I deserve to be**

loved, and so they're drawn towards relationships and situations that reinforce those expectations for them. But if we've been looking at life through a lens that tells us: **Yes, I can be happy, BUT I just have to struggle first to make it happen**, then quite without realising it, we get drawn to situations and relationships that confirm that.

Re-creating, Reinforcing, and Re-experiencing

We all face challenges from time to time. That's how we learn and grow wiser. The problem is that if we continue to view life through a lens that tells us we have to struggle, then rather than learning and moving forward, we get stuck going round in circles. The stuck-ness happens because we expect life to be a certain way, so we recreate the same situations for ourselves, which then reinforce the beliefs that got us there in the first place! It becomes a self-fulfilling prophecy.

It can be very easy to look at a challenging situation or difficult person in our current life and place the responsibility for our unhappiness onto that. The truth is that although a problem can very much *appear* to be caused by a present-day person or situation, it's often just another replay of experiences we've had in the past.

That's a tough concept to take on board, especially if someone else has really hurt us. It can seem that they've come along uninvited and have behaved badly. But the fact is that we'd very likely have experienced that person's behaviour in a very different way, or avoided them altogether, had we had a different set of beliefs about who we are, how other people should treat us, and how life is.

Has there been a problem, an issue, that's come up in your life, again, and again, and again? Is it something that always crops up in your relationships, or with your confidence, or in your working life? If so, you're not alone, but you don't have to continue on reliving these past experiences over and over. Like thousands of people before you, you can learn to recognise the mistaken beliefs that are contributing to your problems, and, you can learn how to let them go and start viewing life through a much happier, and wiser, lens.

Stepping Back from the Struggle Lens

The Four Beliefs

The vast majority of people can't see their own limiting beliefs. It's a bit like they're standing with their nose right up against their lens of the world. They're so close to it that all they can see is a blur. It's only when they take a step back that they get to see the full picture.

Therapy is a bit like taking that step back. In the process of helping many people do just this, I've seen that there are four main limiting beliefs that create the lens of struggle. These beliefs are very common. See if you recognise them as figuring in your own life. The Four Beliefs are:

- » I Must Be Strong
- » I Have To Please People
- » I Need To Prove Myself
- » I Have To Do Everything By Myself

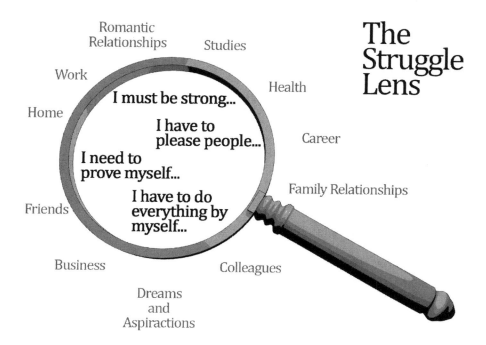

There are two important points to make about these beliefs.

» The first is that these four struggle beliefs are very much related; if we have one of them, it's very likely that, at least to some extent, we'll also have the other three.

» The second is that all struggle beliefs are based on some form of fear.

The reason we tend to approach life in these ways is because we're afraid, at some deep level, that we're not good enough as we are. Interestingly, the word 'afraid' comes from the word 'afeared,' and this is the point—all our limiting beliefs come from a place of fear. Approaching life from a perspective of fear means we're so focused on trying to find love through the approval of others that we often forget it's possible to simply concentrate on loving ourselves.

We'll be looking more at approaching life through either fear or love as we continue on our journey here together. For now, let's explore each of the four struggle beliefs so that you can get a good understanding of how they may be impacting on your life, or maybe the life of someone you know.

I Must Be Strong

Always having to be strong means we're so used to the idea that life is all about enduring hardships that we just carry on trying to cope with what's in front of us, rather than stepping back and considering that there could be other ways of viewing a problem. We don't accept our own vulnerabilities and can be very hard on ourselves—when there's really no need.

And because we're so busy with all this struggling and coping, it can seem easier to ignore our feelings completely, so we squash them down. I've often heard people who hold this belief say they find it hard to cry, or they worry that if they did start crying they wouldn't be able to stop.

Believing we must be strong often means we brush off people's offers of support or guidance, and we say things like 'Oh I'm ok—other people are worse off than me.' And we struggle on, wearing a metaphorical suit of armour, enduring hardships, and we barely notice when life becomes more and more stressful — because being stressed is normal to us.

All this burdensome living means we need to find a way to compensate for our hardships, and common ways we do this is through our unhelpful habits. Cigarettes, alcohol, overeating, overspending or any other 'soother' can appear to be a helpful ally in a harsh and unkind world.

Some of the signs of the 'I Must Be Strong' belief are:

» Unable to get in touch with feelings or ignoring distressing emotions

» Feeling very tired for no real reason

» Finding it hard to give up something when it's clear it's not working

» Having unhelpful habits or addictions

» Having unexplained bouts of feeling low or depressed

Grace's Story

When twenty-seven-year-old Grace came to see me for therapy she was very low indeed. In the past two years she'd put on three and a half stone. She was eating too much, she told me, and all the wrong foods. Grace had also been trying to quit smoking but hadn't been able to. She couldn't go to the shops without spending money on things she didn't really want, and her credit card bills were going through the roof.

Grace felt like she was steadily losing control of her life. She was wise enough to see that she was caught in a cycle — the more she used these unhelpful habits to soothe herself, the more stressed and depressed she became, and so the more she turned to these habits for comfort.

Grace worked in an office as an admin assistant — a job she didn't enjoy, she told me. The job was supposed to have been a fresh start; she'd been ill with stress and had been out of work for over a year before and this was supposed to have been a way to boost her confidence. But Grace was unhappy and unfulfilled. She came home every night and binged on crisps and junk food to compensate for having to endure another miserable day.

Prior to being ill, Grace had been to university. She'd attended for two years, taking a course in Business Studies, but hadn't been able to finish it. She'd never really been interested in Business Studies; she'd only taken on the course to stop her mother worrying. When Grace got stuck on course assignments she'd just struggled on rather than asking for help from her tutor, because she thought that asking would make her look stupid. Grace got so stressed and behind with the coursework that she couldn't catch up. And in the end, she'd had to give it up. Giving up was something that Grace never did — it was a huge setback in her life.

In our early sessions, Grace found it hard to talk about her feelings — her mother had always been so theatrical about everything. Grace had learnt to shut her feelings off and just be practical and resilient in the face of problems and get on with life. She described her mother as a rather helpless sort of person who found it hard to cope with life and Grace had always felt a responsibility to take care of her. In fact, she'd often felt like she was the parent and her mother was the daughter.

Grace enjoyed writing but had never thought of making a career out of it. She was so much in the habit of thinking she had to just handle what life threw at her that she'd never stopped to consider that she had choices. Now, as she began to consider that it could possibly be the way she was viewing life that was the problem, she began to feel excited about the possibility of change. She wondered: could she choose how her life would be? Was it possible that she could create a future for herself of her own making?

When we approach life from the mistaken idea that we 'must be strong', we can easily get caught up in a cycle of forgetting to be kind to ourselves, making life harder and thus reinforcing the idea that we need to be strong.

I Must Be Strong → Forgetting Self-Kindness → Feeling Vulnerable Overwhelmed → Life's a Struggle → (I Must Be Strong)

Once we let go of the idea that we have to battle on, enduring hardships, we start being much kinder to ourselves, and life immediately becomes easier. Allowing ourselves to be vulnerable sometimes is a good thing, not a bad thing. If we're willing to be open and share ourselves with others, we get to have much healthier and supportive relationships. Actually, people like to see someone being real: it gives them permission to be real too!

Maybe you recognise that sometimes you feel the need 'to be strong' too? It's a belief that's common to many. Later, in The Transformation Process, I'll be sharing specific techniques to help let go of this unhelpful belief and start bringing more self-kindness into your life. For now let's look at the second struggle belief — 'I Have to Please People!'

I Have To Please People

I've met many people over the years whose need to please has caused problems in their relationships and with their confidence. The urge to keep other people happy in order to be liked and to avoid rejection can be very strong, but constantly being in 'pleasing mode' ultimately leads to feeling resentful, and often angry.

And those people we're trying to please may well take advantage without even realising they're doing so. Odd as it may sound, even the nicest, most well-meaning of people can disregard a 'pleaser' in this way, and there's a good reason for this—subconscious communication.

A lot of the time we tend to think of communication as being open, and easily recognisable; you say something, I hear it... I say something back, you hear it... and so it goes on. Much of the time though, we communicate indirectly and in subtle ways. We do this by the signals we give each other, through our behaviour and by the way we treat ourselves. People make 'subconscious deals' all the time about what they expect from each other. When we approach life from the belief 'I have to please people,' we unwittingly set up a subliminal agreement that we'll put other's needs before our own. The Pleasing People Agreement goes something like this:

'I will put up with your stuff; you don't need to think about my needs, but I'll always be understanding of your needs and make sure you're OK. Then I can be happy because you'll like me and think I'm a good person and want to be around me.'

Needing to please also tends to create confusion between supporting others and rescuing them. It means life can become quite a struggle because we can end up taking on far too much responsibility for other people's problems. To support someone means empowering them whilst holding true to our own sense of worth; it means helping another person to help themselves. To rescue, on the other hand, means rushing in and doing everything for that person, regardless of our own needs. And this, in the end, doesn't help anyone.

Some of the signs of the 'I Have to Please People' belief are:

» Being unable to fully relax if others aren't happy

» Feeling resentful and angry about never having enough time

» Trying to make a relationship work when the other doesn't put in the effort

» Finding it difficult to say 'No' to people and being taken for granted

» Being caught in the middle of others' problems

Amanda's Story

When Amanda, thirty-nine, arrived for our first session, I noticed how tired she looked. She told me that she felt weighed down by life, and by the way her friends and family behaved towards her.

'I must have "TREAT ME LIKE AN IDIOT" tattooed on my forehead,' she said. 'Why are people so awful to me? I try really hard to be nice, but they still treat me like dirt!'

Amanda described herself as the 'go-between' in her family. Her younger twin sisters and her parents didn't get along at all. They all turned to Amanda to pass on messages between them, and, although they often expected her to sort out their problems, none of them showed her any thanks. It was just assumed she'd be at their beck and call — at least that's how Amanda saw it. She told me, 'I often find myself stuck in the middle and then everyone turns and blames me for their problems!'

Amanda had a teenage daughter, Jo, who spent most of her time storming off to stay with friends because she was angry with her mother for one reason or another. Jo's father had abandoned them when Jo was only a baby. Since then Amanda had had a few relationships, but none of them had worked out. 'They seem to start out really well,' said Amanda, 'but I always find myself being let down.'

I noticed Amanda used the words 'find myself' a lot; it was as though she didn't see herself as in control of her own life; it just 'sort of' happened to her.

With friends, Amanda was eager to give a helping hand; she offered to babysit, she helped them decorate, and she walked people's dogs and looked after their cats. She told me she was always offering to help other people because she thought that they would be nice to her in return. But these friends very often took Amanda for granted. One supposedly good friend, a woman whom Amanda had lent money for a wedding dress, had forgotten to invite Amanda to the wedding! It was the last straw.

Amanda didn't like the negative person she was becoming. She was resentful towards other people for treating her so shoddily and she was angry with herself for letting them do so. She was also worried that if she let her resentment show, it might damage her relationships — some of which she'd been putting a lot of effort into for a long time.

Amanda assumed that she was unhappy because of the way other people treated her. She hadn't ever considered that by looking for validation from other people she was forgetting to look to herself. It was a new way of thinking for Amanda. This realisation helped her feel more empowered. She began to see that instead of seeking happiness outside of herself from other people, she could start from within. Amanda began to see a glimmer of happiness as she understood that by loving herself and valuing herself, she could get the much-needed regard she'd always wanted, and, she could depend on that regard always being there! Amanda began to see light at the end of the tunnel as she considered ways to say 'No,' with kindness, but firmly.

❧❧❧❧❧

Amanda's story is very common. We get so caught up in chasing approval from others that we forget to stop and look at ourselves and remember just how special we are. By forgetting to value ourselves we can easily end up with poor relationships with others, feeling disregarded and disrespected. This just makes us feel even more in a need of validation from outside of ourselves.

If you recognise yourself as a people pleaser then you're not alone. It's a typical limiting belief that causes struggle for many people. Once you let go of the need for validation from others, you'll find your relationship with yourself and with those others will improve greatly and life will become much easier.

Later, in The Transformation Process, I'll be showing you some special techniques and practices to help let go of the need to please, and to help you experience more self-worth in your life. For now, let's look at the third struggle belief — 'I Need to Prove Myself!'

I Need To Prove Myself

I've found that people who tend to approach life with the belief 'I Need to Prove Myself' are often very hard-working and ambitious people who dream big. The problem is that having to prove themselves all the time automatically puts them into struggle mode, because they put so much pressure on themselves to achieve wonderful results all of the time.

All the great achievements in life come about through a creative process of trial and error. We test something out and then resolve what doesn't work — that's how we learn and grow, and become wiser. Yet if we're always worried about proving ourselves as good enough, we can't go through this process because every failure is perceived as a catastrophe and thus provides evidence that we are not good enough. Instead of allowing our creative energy to help us, we block our creativity and sabotage our own progress.

The need to prove often makes itself known to us in our working life when we try to show that we're indispensable. It means we work ridiculously hard, often trying to cover all tasks and forgetting to share or outsource work.

Never feeling quite good enough means that we tend to spend a lot of time carrying on an inner dialogue of self-criticism. Basically, we are mean to ourselves! And quite without realising it, we can put pressure on people around us, making them feel inadequate too. Needing to prove tends to drive people away because there's always some level of stress happening.

Some of the signs of the 'I Need to Prove Myself' belief are:

» Spending a lot of time firefighting problems

» Working really hard but never seeming to get to where you want to be in life

» Wondering why life is such a struggle when others have it easier

» Feeling stressed and overwhelmed by 'all the things you have to do'

» Comparing yourself to others: either deciding you're better than they are or not as good as they are

Theo's Story

Theo, fifty-one, looked hesitant as he came into the room and sat down opposite me. I smiled reassuringly, and asked how I could help him. He said, 'My wife and sons want me to get help for my confidence. They think there's something wrong; I guess I haven't been happy for a long time.'

In that first session, Theo talked a great deal; his words seemed to bubble up and tumble over each other in his eagerness to get them out and I became aware that he kept jumping from one topic to another. Changing the subject is something people often do when they fear disapproval: it's a way of not 'staying in one place for too long,' and therefore not leaving enough time for the listener to form judgements about them.

And in his life, too, Theo had found it hard to settle. He'd worked in various jobs but didn't stay long in any of them, he told me, because of his nerves. He had also set up a number of small businesses which he described as having failed because he'd run out of time or money. All of this had happened, despite him working all hours and running things on a shoestring. Theo seemed proud to tell me how he'd struggled through his businesses, doing every aspect of the work himself, from the accounts, to the designs. His businesses, in website design, photography, and online marketing, had all started out well, and he'd been full of enthusiasm, but something always seemed to go wrong despite his great efforts. From his point of view, Theo had always worked extra hard, but life had just come along unfairly and sabotaged his success.

In one of our sessions, Theo told me that he volunteered for a local charity. He loved the project, helping the elderly, but he often worried that the staff thought he wasn't doing enough. I could see how important other people's opinions were to him; he needed acceptance but that was something he never felt he had enough of, no matter how hard he tried to prove he was good enough.

I noticed that Theo spent a lot of time criticising and judging himself for his perceived failures. When I pointed this out to him, he said 'Oh yes, I always do that.' It was a habit Theo was aware of; he just wasn't aware how much it was impacting on his life.

There was a period of time, during our sessions, when Theo felt quite despondent as he came to see that he'd been sabotaging his own success by pressurising himself so much. He continued beating himself up with comments about his 'wasted time'. But soon he began to acknowledge that it was a good thing to recognise his tendency to need to prove himself — now he could work on letting go of his self-inflicted pressure and look to the future.

He began to wonder, could he possibly make a success of his life simply by letting go? Could he learn to like himself more, to accept himself, just as he was?

৶৶৶৶৶

We all want to feel good about ourselves and to make a success of our lives — of course! But having the mistaken idea that we have to keep proving ourselves doesn't help. It's not loving ourselves at all; it sabotages us rather than helping us, because we're inclined to judge and criticise ourselves and so the need to prove becomes even more persistent.

When we let go of the need to prove ourselves, life tends to improve quickly. That's because as soon as we stop trying to prove ourselves, we start accepting ourselves. The opinion of others becomes much less important; and funnily enough that's exactly when others start accepting us all the more — because we're showing them what love and acceptance really looks like and we all enjoy being reminded of that.

It's in this state of allowing ourselves to love ourselves that we start tuning in with our creative energy; that's when solutions to the little challenges of life make their way to us; that's when inspiration and 'aha' moments happen for us. Then we begin to form new beliefs about how easy life can be and we begin to acknowledge all the good things we accomplish each day. In The Transformation Process, I'll be sharing specific techniques and methods to help let go of the need to prove and to replace it with lots of self-acceptance and love. For now, let's look at the last of the four struggle beliefs — 'I Have To Do Everything By Myself!'

I Have To Do Everything By Myself

When we believe we have to do everything by ourselves, it's because we fear that if we share our worries and problems, people may think we're weak, and may reject us as not being good enough in some way. This makes it very hard to ask for support; in fact the bigger the problem, the more likely we are to struggle on alone.

Even if we do consider asking for help, we quickly dismiss the idea because we don't know how to go about asking in a way that will save face. We're also unsure of who to trust because we're so unfamiliar with sharing our needs with others. We get so much in to the habit of dealing with problems alone, that people are often surprised when they discover we've been struggling! Trying to show we can do everything by ourselves can make it look like we're, at best, fine as we are, or, at worst, arrogant and unfriendly. Have you ever met someone who seemed a bit aloof, only to discover later that they're actually a really lovely person? It's likely that they're approaching life from this belief.

Some of the signs of the 'I Have To Do Everything By Myself' belief are:

» Finding it hard to trust in the support of others

» Having anxiety attacks and stress-related physical ailments

» Fearing people's scorn if a mistake is made

» Working extra-long hours or taking work home

» Feeling like a failure for needing to share tasks

David's Story

Twenty-one-year-old David came for help with his panic attacks. They were so severe that he felt he had no choice but to seek help. It was so bad that he was beginning to make excuses not to go into work. David had been lucky to get a placement on a trainee scheme with a major bank the year before. The future had looked promising then, but now he was really worried that he might lose his job. He hadn't told anyone about his anxiety; he didn't want to look like he couldn't cope and he didn't know who he could trust at work to talk to.

David described himself as having been a 'bit of a loner' when he was growing up. He'd struggled at school and hadn't gone on to university as had many of his peers. Now he was finding it hard to fit in with his colleagues at the bank; a number of them were older, with more experience, and David fretted and worried that he didn't measure up.

He worked long hours and frequently worked through lunch because he wanted his manager to notice how dedicated and responsible he was. He'd been getting through each week in a constant bubble of stress and was frequently tired and on edge—it was no wonder he was so anxious!

David was immensely proud of his father, who had worked extremely hard to build up his own business as an accountant. The family had wanted for nothing: expensive holidays, private schools for David and his two sisters, the best clothes, the best of everything. Unfortunately, his father had had to retire early due to poor health. As the only son, David felt that he should follow his father's example and show he could be a man. He was determined to stand on his own two feet and make a success of life by himself.

David very often used the phrase 'being a man.' He was ashamed of his panic attacks; he considered them to be a sign that he didn't measure up in some way, so he'd been resolutely carrying on without help. But his determination hadn't got him anywhere; his anxiety had just got worse and now he was sitting in front of me, having to share his worries and feelings of vulnerability. I was compelled to point out to David that it was a sign of courage on his part, rather than failure, to come for help.

My encouragement was something David found hard to accept at first. But in time he began to acknowledge that his need to do everything by himself was more of a hindrance than a help.

He told me in one session that he was upset because someone at work had called him arrogant—he didn't see himself like this at all. He hadn't realised that he was coming across as so unfriendly and distant; he was just in his own 'world of worry' all the time.

David began to see that all the pressure he'd been putting himself under at work had turned small daily tasks into huge problems and stress. He saw that the cause of his anxiety was his attitude to work — not the work itself. He began to wonder what would happen if he starting sharing tasks and asking for help? Could it be that no one would think any less of him?

ॐॐॐॐॐ

This need to show we can 'do it alone' is a common mistake. Many of us wander through life, struggling on alone, and thinking this will make us more confident. But in the long run, this lack of self-loving creates pressure and erodes our confidence, rather than boosting it.

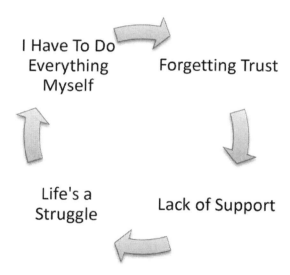

I Have To Do Everything Myself

Forgetting Trust

Life's a Struggle

Lack of Support

Once we let go of this idea (and I'll be showing you how to do so), life becomes so much better — we begin to pull people towards us rather than pushing them away. We start to enjoy the great benefits of reciprocity, and, as we begin giving and receiving equally in relationships, we start to feel more confident and trusting.

The stories and struggles I've been sharing are common for many of us. I've experienced some of them, and I'm guessing that you've identified with some of them too. They're the sort of problems that keep popping up in our lives in different situations and with different people, and it's no wonder they keep coming back, because our limiting beliefs keep us caught up in these cycles of fear and lack of self-love. When we're stuck like this, it can feel as though life will always be a struggle. But it doesn't have to be like this. We can learn to let go of these fear-based beliefs. Then we can reverse the cycle, and when fear is absent from our lives we can make so much more room for love.

But Wait a Minute! Struggling can be Very Compelling!

It certainly seems like a good idea to let go of these four limiting beliefs. So why not just do that? Why not simply make the decision to start thinking and behaving in more positive, helpful ways and get on with life? What stops us from letting go of our struggles and starting to love ourselves a little more?

As an ex-struggler myself, I just want to acknowledge something here. Whilst I've been speaking of the benefits of letting go of these limiting beliefs, I also know that struggling with life can feel very compelling and even appealing.

Acknowledging this is HUGELY important if we're going to be able to let those beliefs go.

You see, every time a problem such as a difficult relationship or a demanding work load comes up in life, we can feel an excited anticipation that 'here is a chance to prove ourselves good enough to cope with it!' Strange as this may sound, struggling can feel compelling — almost addictive — and this is the reason why we continue on, stuck in these limiting beliefs, even when they make us unhappy. If we're to be successful in letting them go, we first need to understand why it can be so compelling to hold onto them. And it all starts with where they came from.

When you were a child, you tottered and toddled around the frontiers of your world and you looked up and took great note of those bigger people and what they had to teach you.

Chapter Three
How We Learnt to Struggle

*'I am a beloved child of the Universe and the
Universe lovingly takes care of me now and forever more.'*
Louise Hay

None of us arrives into this world alone. When you were born, there was at the very least one other person around for you: your mother. It's likely that there were others too: your father, other family members, and family friends, all eager to welcome you into the world. You were a new little person to care for, and as your mentors, those people held the honourable task of guiding you and letting you know that you were cherished and supported and loved.

The early days of your life were fairly straightforward. You weren't aware of much, except that you got hungry and thirsty and you needed shelter, cuddles, and reassurance. At that point in your life you didn't feel a need to prove anything to anyone. There was no requirement to try to keep other people happy or earn your way into their affection.

Time passed. You matured from babyhood to toddlerhood, and as you became a fully-fledged little person in the world you became increasingly aware of your surroundings: people, places, buildings, trees, furniture… and everything was big!

From your perspective, as that small person, buildings seemed to stretch right into the sky, trees seemed like flowers that hadn't stopped growing, furniture was a fantastic obstacle course, and people towered over you. You tottered and toddled around the frontiers of your world and you looked up and took great note of those bigger people and what they had to teach you.

Big People: Big Messages

Those people made a very significant impression on you; not only were they big in stature, they were *big* in the influence they had over you. They taught you everything. They helped you learn how to walk and to talk and what to eat. They taught you about colours, what words and numbers meant, and they showed you everything about the world in which you lived. You absorbed everything. You paid great attention, not only to the words those bigger people used, but their tone of voice, their moods, their body language, and how they behaved. All this information became the messages that led you to conclude what life was about and what you should expect your place to be in the world.

It's those people who greatly influenced the lens through which you would look at life from then on. Some of their messages to you were of course wonderful — you were treated with love and affection, given attention, and regarded as a treasured and worthy little person. And some of their messages were not so good at all.

Of course it's inevitable that some of the messages you received as a child were less than helpful to your emotional well-being. The adults in your life were most likely busy, perhaps juggling work and family, trying to fulfil their own needs and everyone else's. So it's only natural that some friction occurred and you ended up feeling hurt and disappointed. Along with this, those adults were operating from the lens they had formed in their own childhood, so the messages they passed on to you, whilst full of good intention, may have been negative and therefore had a negative impact on you.

These messages may have been communicated via the adults' words, but they could have just as easily been communicated through their behaviours. Their actions, and inactions, which seemed of little importance to them at the time, may well have had a lasting impact on you at such an impressionable age. A cross look, a bad-tempered comment, or failure to respond to your requests were important in your life. These experiences may have been isolated events, or there may have been a number of repeated negative experiences that made a deep impression on you. Either way they will have led you to question your own worth — maybe even your security.

Here are a few examples that the clients in this book remembered. Maybe you have similar recollections?

» The teacher glared and shouted at me

» Granddad told me 'big boys don't cry'

» Mum and Dad were too busy arguing to notice me

» They forgot my lunch money

» Mum told me I was a mistake

Little Children's Theta Waves

But why do these early experiences create such an impact on small children?

It's not by chance. A small child's brainwaves function in Theta state, and this is very different to the Beta state of an adult's brainwaves. Theta brainwaves of children aged from about two to seven years old vibrate at a specific frequency, between 4 Hz and 8 Hz, a bit like when an adult is under hypnosis. This allows children to absorb a great deal of information from the external world without questioning it — it helps them learn and develop quickly. This makes perfect sense; that period of development from babyhood to age seven is filled with so much to take in; it's very important that all that information gets into a child's brain easily and for it to be firmly stored there.

So small children quite naturally take in every piece of information they're presented with and believe it to be completely true. This is why they so easily believe in Father Christmas and magical characters such as Superman or Harry Potter. Their brain is not yet set up to start reasoning and asking questions about the meaning of what they're told, or what they observe. So just as they believe that Father Christmas comes with presents each year, so they believe all the messages they're given about themselves and about other people, whether those messages be positive or negative, funny or scary, happy or sad.

Although parents generally make every effort to create happy experiences and foster positive attitudes in their children, they can't help but contribute to the formation of some limiting beliefs too. Say, for example, a tired, grumpy parent who has had a hard day at work tells off a child for pestering them. That child may get upset and even cry.

Then maybe they'll appear to quickly recover from their distress. If you've ever spent time with a little one, you may have noticed how they can be in tears one minute, and the next minute they're off playing and giggling as if nothing had ever happened.

But these experiences — words, tone of voice, facial expressions, body language, behaviours — are all pieces of information which that child absorbs into their subconscious, along with a 'physical memory' such as a pounding heart, tightness in the throat, a churning stomach … and all of this will resurface in future times of stress.

Both forms of information, cognitive and physical, combine and are locked into what we call the body-mind. The way your heart pounds when you take an exam today, first happened when you were a child and had a stressful experience of being tested in some way. Your body has remembered that for all these years!

This Just Isn't Right!

But, whilst children are biologically set up to absorb those messages as true, there's also something else afoot: something deeper, at their soul level. Every child comes into the world with an innate awareness: they know that they're part of the powerful, magical force of life — a power which can only ever be giving and loving and accepting of them.

So if a child is frequently given messages that tell them they're not good enough, that they don't deserve support, acceptance and love, well, they know deep down that that's not right—that simply isn't how it's supposed to be!

Perhaps you can remember a time in your own childhood when you were judged harshly or felt abandoned or unloved? Do you remember thinking, 'It's not fair!' Perhaps the harsh judgement seemed uncalled for, because you knew on some deeper level that you were good, and that you deserved to be accepted, not unaccepted; that you deserved to be treated with kindness, not made to feel unloved. So how do children deal with this conflict between what they know in their hearts, and the negative messages they're being presented with? They come up with a solution to make it feel better!

Every Current Problem Was Once a Solution

The problems we experience in our adult life, very often have their roots in the solutions we came up with as children to try to manage life. When children receive negative messages about themselves, it contradicts their innate sense of their own worth—and that hurts! They have to find some way to deal with that hurt, so they come up with ways of thinking and behaving which will make the situation better. These are the bargains that little children make with life in order to get their need for security and love met in the best way possible. These solutions very often have some condition attached, such as having to prove themselves, endure hardship, and please others. These solutions are the seeds of those troublesome beliefs which will later cause them struggle in adult life. But at the time they're created, these solutions are completely appropriate and in fact very clever ways to adapt to feeling unloved. Children live very much in the moment; they're not considering how life is going to be next year, nor are they considering the consequences of starting a habit of thinking and behaving in ways that will create stress and struggle further down the line—they're simply trying to emotionally survive in the *now*. So they come up with ideas about how to get the love they want—in the *now*.

Here are some examples:

The Problem:

'They seem too busy with their own worries to notice when I'm unhappy. If I cry they tell me off.'

The Solution:

'I'll try really hard not to let my feelings hurt. When I'm upset I'll do something else instead. I'll find something that makes me feel better.'

Belief:

I Must Be Strong

The Problem:

'Mum and Dad don't seem to like me very much. They're always yelling at each other: they tell me off or ignore me.'

The Solution:

'I'll be really good, and then they'll have to like me. I'll be nice to everyone, and make sure they are ok, and I won't ever get angry or show I'm upset.'

Belief:

I have to please people.

The Problem:

'Whatever I do, it's never good enough. They've got more time for (brother/sister). They only pay attention to me when I do something special.'

The Solution:

'I'll try harder; I need to prove that I'm really special and then I'll get them to love me.'

Belief:

I need to prove myself.

The Problem:

'Mum and Dad get cross when I tell them I'm upset. They never cuddle me.'

The Solution:

'I can't trust those people to be there for me. I'd better not trust anyone; they'll probably let me down. I'll just rely on myself from now on.'

Belief:

I Have To Do Everything By Myself.

The following four stories may remind you of experiences, past or recent, when you too felt compelled to think and act on these beliefs. Remember to jot those memories down in your notebook. This will be useful later, when we work with The Transformation Process. If nothing comes to mind — no worries, I'll be providing you with an exercise to help you identify significant memories to work on.

Little Grace's Solution

Grace was well aware that her overeating and overspending was causing even more problems for herself — she just didn't know how to stop. When I asked her how long she'd been doing this, she told me that food had always been an issue. As far back as she could remember she'd eaten for comfort. She recalled being about three or four years old. Whenever her mother was downstairs shouting at her father on the phone Grace would get under her bedcovers and eat sweets to try to stop herself feeling sad. She remembered a time when her mother came into her room and told her that her daddy was mean and didn't give them enough money, and then gave her a bar of chocolate to make it all better.

Not long after, Grace's father moved to Italy with his new wife and her two daughters; little Grace was absolutely certain that her daddy didn't love her anymore.

In our sessions, Grace recalled her mother as always upset and crying and not seeming to notice when Grace herself was upset or needed help. Her mother was often too lost in her own problems to listen to her so Grace gave up trying to get comfort from her. She remembered that she'd been frightened by the creaking noises that came from her bedroom radiator at night, but she didn't tell her mother. And she remembered that she'd often had trouble tying her shoelaces in the mornings, but she never asked her mother for help.

Grace recalled another time when she was about seven, and her mother had a new boyfriend, who looked a bit like Father Christmas with his long beard. Grace liked him a lot. It was Christmastime and little Grace had dreamed that he would bring her lots of presents and nice things to eat, but he didn't turn up for their Christmas dinner and Mum got very upset. Grace had just sat in her room eating a packet of chocolate biscuits.

She remembered also, when she was fourteen, that she'd had a holiday in Italy with her father and stepmother and two stepsisters. It was very relaxed there and Grace picked up smoking from her older sisters. No one seemed to mind her smoking. In fact, her father didn't pay her much attention at all. He barely seemed to notice she was there. Grace tried to be strong and not show how hurt she was.

Looking back, Grace realised that she must have concluded from very early on that life was something to be struggled through. She hadn't been able to depend on anyone to be there for her in any consistent way. So she had come up with a very resourceful solution for a small girl of only four years old — she would be strong. She would carry on and take care of herself and she would use sweets to help her feel better. As Grace got older, she added junk food, cigarettes, and shopping to this self-soothing habit. She continued approaching everything in her life with an 'I must be strong' attitude, being unkind and harsh on herself — without even realising she was doing so.

Little Amanda's Solution

Amanda found it hard to say 'No' when her friends and family asked her for help or when they dumped their problems on her. The more they took her for granted, the more she was driven to try to please them. I asked her if it had always been this way, and, when she thought about it, she realised that she'd been doing this as far back as she could remember.

Life had been traumatic in her childhood. Her parents were frequently at loggerheads, and from an early age Amanda had become their go-between. She remembered one time, when she was about five years old. Her mother said, 'Tell your father his dinner's going in the bin if he doesn't get home on time tonight.' Amanda had forgotten to tell him and when he didn't come home for dinner that evening, her mother became so angry that she threw all the dinner plates on the floor. Little Amanda had thought it was her fault for not reminding him.

Her father, a chronic gambler who seemed powerless over his addiction, was an angry man. He was often angry with little Amanda too, as she always seemed to be around when he was in a low mood. She remembered when she was six; he'd smacked her bottom and said, **'I wish you would just go away!'**

And then the twins arrived. Little Amanda, only seven years old, looked after them even though she was scared when they screamed and she didn't know what to do. Mum and Dad were always in another room shouting about money. Somewhere along the line she decided that if she tried very hard and looked after the babies, then Mum and Dad would be happier, and if they were happy, they would be nice to her. And they were, sometimes.

Amanda continued to try hard to please her parents; she nodded wisely when Mum complained about Dad and listened carefully when Dad complained about Mum. She was on her best behaviour as much as she could be and she took care of everyone's needs. When she was ten years old, Amanda had a lovely teacher, who really encouraged her. She worked extra hard to make him happy by drawing pictures for him and practising her spelling; it felt good when the teacher was nice to her.

So from a very young age, Amanda had come up with a clever solution for such a little girl—if she kept people happy, they would like her and be nice to her. It was hard work, but she'd been carrying on like this ever since, completely unaware of the signals she was giving people about her sense of unworthiness and how she expected to be treated.

Little Theo's Solution

Theo could clearly see that his need to prove himself had started in his childhood. Looking back, he remembered himself as a quiet child, especially compared to his brother Frank, who was older than Theo by four years. Frank was something that the grown-ups called a 'tearaway,' a word which little Theo didn't understand. He thought it meant that his brother would tear away his bedroom wallpaper when he was having one of his angry times.

Theo's parents very often had to go to the school to talk to the teachers about some problem of Frank's. They spent a lot of time talking about Frank at home, too. Sometimes they were so distracted that they forgot to give Theo his lunch money. They didn't listen to him when he talked about things that mattered to him. In those times Theo felt as though he was invisible to them. He recalled how he used to worry that one day they would forget he was there, move house and leave him behind!

Theo's mother once told him that he had been 'a mistake' — another phrase which little Theo didn't quite understand — but he got the message that he'd not been wanted.

By the time he was seven, Theo realised that Frank got lots of attention because he was naughty, so Theo started to be naughty too. It wasn't nice when Dad shouted at him and sent him to his room, but it was good that Dad had noticed he was there. Other times, Theo would try to be very, very good and Mum would give him a smile, which lit up his heart.

When Theo was eight, his parents arranged a birthday party for him and he invited all his friends from school. Theo was ecstatically proud and happy, but they cancelled it at the last minute. Mum was just too upset — the police had brought Frank home after he'd been caught shoplifting. For weeks after, Theo's classmates teased him and laughed about his 'Not Party.'

In the back of his mind, Theo always had the idea that one day, things would change. He imagined Frank going away somewhere and never coming back, and he imagined his mum holding out her arms for a hug and his dad smiling and asking how his day at school had been.

As he grew older, Theo worked really hard at school. He joined lots of clubs so that he could impress his dad with some new achievement. His teachers often complimented him on his hard work and Theo lapped up their attention. Without even being aware of it, little Theo had made the decision that if he was going to earn acceptance and love he would have to work extra hard to prove he was good enough. He'd been carrying on like this all through the years, not realising that this constant struggling for approval was at the root of many of the problems in his life.

Little David's Solution

David's anxiety was threatening to ruin his career at the bank. I wondered how long he'd been feeling so stressed. On reflection, David couldn't recall a time when he'd ever been completely at ease in his life.

He told me about his childhood. His father had been distant and aloof, often busy working with little time to spend with the family. His mother stayed at home. She spent a lot of her time looking after David's two younger sisters. I pictured David as having been a rather lonely child in the midst of all this. He agreed.

David was often left in the care of his grandfather, a somewhat stern person who frowned a lot. He had been a young soldier in World War II; he often told little David stories about horrible injuries and death which frightened him.

David recalled one day when he was about four years old; he'd fallen on some rough ground at the park and had scraped his knees quite badly and was crying. He remembered quite clearly that his grandfather had frowned and said, **'Big boys don't cry!'** Then, he had taken him home, patched up his knee and told him not to bother his mother with it because she had other things to think about with his little sisters.

As David recounted this to me, another memory popped into his head. He was seven years old, at school. He'd put up his hand to answer the teacher's question, but his answer had been wrong and the teacher had said, 'Oh, no, David!' and all the other children had laughed at him. David had been so embarrassed and distressed by this. Later, when he told his mother, she said, 'Don't be silly, David! Keep a stiff upper lip: that's the British way.'

'Actually,' David told me, 'she's been saying that for years!'

In time, little David learnt that showing feelings was not a good idea. This was especially true when he felt scared and vulnerable, because at those times, people either didn't have the patience for him or they frowned upon him for being needy.

At that young age, David didn't understand the concept of struggle. Yet already, deep in his subconscious, he'd already decided to view the world through the messages he was receiving from those important people in his life—'Don't share your feelings', 'Don't be vulnerable,' 'Get on with things by yourself.'

These messages weren't new; they had been passed down through the generations, from David's grandfather to his own son, David's father, and now on to David. And so in a completely different century and circumstances, little David had come to view the world through the same lens—life was a struggle. If he were to get the love and ac-ceptance he craved, he would have to keep his worries hidden and get on with things all by himself.

ৡৡৡৡৡৡ

All children want to be loved and to feel happy. It makes sense then, that if they're not getting that love and happiness, they'll try out different ways to make it happen. Children experiment until they find something that works, such as pleasing people, enduring hardships, or proving themselves, and if certain solutions work well, they carry on with them. These become what psychologists call their 'core be-liefs.' When a few core beliefs are grouped together, a lens begins to form through which all of life is viewed. And as we've seen, many of us view life through the lens of struggle.

The Most Mistaken Belief in the World

Over the years I've helped hundreds of people recognise their ten-dency to approach life from beliefs about struggle. In that time, I've come to clearly understand that there's one main limiting belief that underpins all the others.

This belief is a deeply ingrained misunderstanding. It's a mistaken notion that's been passed down from generation to generation, and it's the single, most unhelpful idea that's ever existed. That belief is:

I Can Be Separated From Love

Of course, looking at the bigger picture, this seems like a strange idea. How could it possibly be true? We're all part of a universe run by an intelligent and nurturing power; a power that's kind and supportive and gives us life. It's loving in its very nature—we wouldn't all be here, otherwise! So where did we get this mistaken idea that we could possibly be separated from that love?

It's quite simple really; it's because of the concept of separation itself. In order to experience human life, we need this thing we call separation so that we can have contrasting experiences. As we've seen, we're wisdom seekers — that's our buzz! Contrast gives us the chance to expand, to become wiser, to figure out how life works by choosing what we do want, what we don't want, and how to make that all come together for a satisfying life.

We're aware of contrast from the very beginning. Even as tiny infants we see that there's a *this way*, and a *that way* about how life works. We get hungry, then we're full; we feel cold, then we're warm again; we need to be cuddled and then we are held and comforted. We continue on through life with this understanding that there can *be something* or *not be something*, and, even though this difference can be challenging for us at times, it's a good thing because contrast offers us options and choices so that we can learn and grow wiser.

But there's a problem.

The problem is that we've mistakenly come to the conclusion that it's the same for love. We think that love is a thing of contrast too: something that we can *have* or *not have*; something that we can obtain or be separated from. And because we've got this mistaken idea, deep down, we worry that we won't be able to get hold of enough love, or that we might lose the love we already have. This worry leads us to believe that we have to work really, really hard for love. We think that the only way we can be sure of having it is to earn it through the approval of others. When we make this mistake, we turn love into a commodity. It becomes something that's scarce — our likelihood of having it is very much dependent on others and how much love they believe they have, or want, to give us.

This is the big mistaken belief that all our struggle beliefs stem from. Love isn't something we can *ever* be separated from. Love isn't something that belongs to other people. It's not even something that we ourselves can own exclusively. Love is a form of energy; a powerful intelligent energy (as we'll shortly be seeing), which exists within each of us. We can't be cut off from it!

It's time to let go of this mistaken notion. Instead of giving each other messages that love is conditional on another's approval, it's much more helpful to remind ourselves of its constant presence within.

We Need Only Come Back to Love

In my own journey out of struggle, I realised that many of the beliefs that had been dictating my life had very little relevance to me as a person. They were deep-rooted, fearful ideas based on the cultural memes of generations of my family before me: generations who'd lived in a different country and who'd had a very different experience of the world than I did. I remember a feeling of lightness coming over me as I began to see that I could simply let it all go: all that time I'd been carrying around a heavy rucksack that didn't belong to me at all — I could simply put it down.

And as I put down that rucksack I saw that there was no need to prove or earn my way into love; I *was* loveable, and I began to see evidence of that love. I saw it in my better relationships because I no longer craved approval. I saw it in my creative approach to life which was no longer blocked by fear and I saw it in my growing wisdom and self-acceptance.

Those ideas about struggling for love that we've all been passing down through the centuries — they were only ever a temporary fix. They don't bring true and lasting happiness: they keep us stuck. It's time now to seek out new ways of being, new solutions to the challenges of life. It's time to change our beliefs.

Have you ever noticed that when you have some sort of conflict or stress with someone you feel powerless and small? One minute you're the competent grown-up, the next you feel tongue-tied and unsure of yourself?

Chapter Four
Why it's So Hard to Change

'I believe the greatest problem we face is that we think we are running our lives with the wishes, desires, and aspirations created by our conscious mind.'

Bruce Lipton

There's an old saying that if you want to know where you're going, you have to know where you're coming from. It's like that with limiting beliefs: once we discover them it's very empowering — now we know there's a possibility for change. As I mentioned, when I realised myself that I simply didn't have to struggle with life anymore, it felt very liberating. Yet my limiting beliefs didn't just disappear because I saw they were there and wished them away. I had to take certain actions to clear them in order to become the happy person I am today.

Changing our beliefs to change our life sounds easy. It's certainly true that knowing where we're coming from gives us self-awareness and that's a great start. But it can be hard to take that self-knowledge and do something about it. I've seen all too often that people reach this point and then get stuck again. They understand *why* they think and behave as they do; they see that their need to please and prove and earn acceptance is sabotaging their relationships, their confidence, their work, and they can clearly see the logic and benefits of ridding themselves of these limiting beliefs ... but still they find it so hard to let them go.

So what's to be done about it? The answer lies in understanding the two main blocks to letting go of these unwanted beliefs, and then taking the appropriate action to remedy that.

The two main blocks are:

» The Subconscious
» The Little Child Within

The Subconscious

Have you ever suddenly remembered something that happened many years ago, and been amazed that it just seemed to pop into your head out of nowhere? It came from your subconscious, where it has been stored all this time, until you re-called it.

Understanding the influence of the subconscious is essential in letting go of our unwanted beliefs. Dr Bruce Lipton, author, cell biologist, and epigeneticist, has written a number of books on how our beliefs affect our life experiences. I can highly recommend his book, *The Biology of Belief: Unleashing the Power of Consciousness, Matter & Miracles*, and I've listed some of his other books in 'Resources' for you. Dr Lipton describes our 'two minds': the conscious mind and the subconscious mind. The conscious mind, he says, is the one connected to our spirit; it's the one that's creative. It's the conscious mind that we use to ask ourselves how we want the story of our life to be, what we want, don't want, our wishes and desires. It's the conscious mind that says 'Enough of being unhappy! I'm ready to change my life now!'

The subconscious mind, however, runs our behaviour and our biology for ninety-five per cent of the time. We can think of the subconscious as something similar to a hard drive on a computer. Our beliefs are the programs, which contain all those experiences we absorbed as children and the ideas and solutions we came up with. Our subconscious then is pretty much running the show!

Imagine a person: let's call him Fred. Fred wakes up in the morning and says to himself,

'Right! Today, I'm going to cause problems, difficulties, and complications for myself. I'm going to go into work and spend the day trying to prove myself beyond what is reasonable. That will stifle my creativity so I'll end up stuck, making mistakes, and feeling bad about myself. I'm going to forget all about my own self-worth and run around after everyone else keeping them all happy. I'll take responsibility for everyone else's problems but I won't share any of my own problems with anyone because it's a really good idea to try and do everything all by myself! Life will be such a struggle!'

Put like that it doesn't sound like Fred is being very kind to himself, does it? Yet in our own way this is just how many of us treat ourselves, unwittingly, because of those programmed struggle beliefs in our subconscious. It doesn't matter that those beliefs started in childhood and are irrelevant to our life as an adult — the subconscious doesn't know that we've grown up now and that life is very different. For the subconscious, there's no difference between past and present: everything is simply 'in the now.' It doesn't know any different. Unlike the conscious mind, it doesn't have the option of making choices and decisions.

But This Is All I Know!

Whenever we make a decision to be a little kinder, more accepting, more loving towards ourselves, it's our conscious mind that makes that choice. For example, we may think:

> **You know what? I'm fed up with trying to prove myself all the time, I'm good enough as I am, I do a good job.**

> **Putting all this pressure on myself just isn't helping. In fact it's just making me feel so stressed that I can't think straight.**

> **I'm so glad I realised. I'll stop now!**

But our subconscious is saying:

> **But this is all I know! This is what I do! I learnt this, and this is what my program is. So I'm just going to keep thinking and behaving like this, over and over and over...**

So we end up frustrated because even though we know *how* to make life better for ourselves, we can't seem to maintain it for long because those darn beliefs are lodged in there. Wouldn't it be great if we could just gently get into the subconscious and release those unwanted beliefs? If we could do that we would find it much easier to treat ourselves with more kindness and consideration. Letting go of our fears and loving ourselves more would mean our relationships would improve, our work would be more inspired and creative, and life would be less struggle, and more happiness and ease.

I just want to pause to make a reassuring point here. If you've ever found it difficult to maintain being more loving towards yourself, it's really important not to judge yourself or blame yourself for that. Knowing that your subconscious has had such an important impact on your life is hopefully a big help in explaining why you've found it difficult.

The Little Child Within

The second reason that we can find it so hard to change is because of the little child within. Every single one of us has a little child within, no matter what age we are—from our teens to our eighties, and beyond. That little child, who first came up with the idea that if they worked really hard to prove themselves, be strong, keep others happy, etc., is still there within each of us, doing their very best to keep us safe in the world. This is why it's often so compelling to keep on thinking and behaving in the old ways of struggle: because they are there, at the ready, being the hero for us.

Let's try a little experiment here. Look at the following table. In the left-hand column we have a list of the four beliefs that create struggle. In the right-hand column are some typical examples of more helpful ways of approaching life. Read the statements in the right-hand column (aloud if you can). Really tune in to what those statements are saying and what it would be like to live in those ways. As you do so, become aware of the sensations in your body. Notice the thoughts that pop into your mind.

Struggle Belief	Much More Helpful Beliefs
I Must Be Strong	Its ok to be vulnerable sometimes. I can trust people to be there for me
I Have To Please People	It's alright to say 'No' to people's requests I'm entitled to voice my opinions
I Need To Prove Myself	I have nothing to prove; I'm good enough just as I am I don't worry about what people think of me
I Have To Do Everything By Myself	I don't have to endure hardships alone Asking for help is a sign of confidence

What came up for you as read those phrases? Did you notice some level of discomfort — a little fear? Perhaps your heart fluttered, your stomach churned, your shoulders got tense? Perhaps you noticed some 'Yes, but' thoughts popping into your mind? Why would that happen? After all, those more helpful ways of approaching life are very good ideas; it would be great to live from that perspective; you'd certainly find life easier, and happier. So why the fear?

There's a very important point to make here. Often when I do this exercise with clients, they point out that the more helpful beliefs in the right-hand column seem much more adult to them. And of course as we've seen, those limiting beliefs about struggle in the left-hand column begin in our childhood.

When we consider approaching life from these more adult, logical and self-loving ways, the fear we feel — the heart fluttering, the stomach churning, the tension building — is the little child within. That little child is scared to surrender their struggling ways and start trusting life in the adult world. It's frightening for them; they've been wearing a suit of armour and have been the hero all this time, helping us 'get through life' by thinking and behaving in these struggle ways. Why would they want to give that up? So when we consider change, they fret and worry:

> 'What if I start saying "No" to people? Will they think I'm mean? Will they stop liking me?'

> 'What if I stop trying to prove myself? Will people think I'm stupid? Will people still like me? Will they think I'm good enough?'

> 'What if I start asking for help? Will people think I'm weak? Will they turn me away? Will I be loved ... wanted ... safe?'

We can know that they're there and that they're worried because of the uncomfortable physical feelings we experience whenever we consider approaching life differently. This is the language of the little child within.

How Old Do I Feel Right Now?

Have you ever noticed that when you have some sort of conflict with someone you feel powerless and small? One minute you're the competent grown-up, the next you feel tongue-tied and unsure of yourself? That's because when we become stressed, we quite naturally, at an emotional level, return to our vulnerable child self. Emotionally we see our self as *small* and the other person as *big*, because when we were a child we actually *were* smaller. So when you're feeling stressed and you find yourself thinking and behaving in ways that don't serve you, a really handy tip is to stop and ask yourself:

> 'How old do I feel right now?'

The chances are your answer will be somewhere between two and nine years old. You'll recognise that it's your little child within who's trying to protect you from rejection or disapproval by trying to prove or please their way out of the situation at hand.

What clever little children we all were to come up with those solutions once upon a time! Now though, in the adult world, it's awfully hard for that little one to be taking on so much responsibility. Little children aren't cut out to deal with the challenges of grown-up life. Imagine a small child going to work, or running a business, or trying to communicate effectively with adult friends! But this is what many of us are trying to do every day. The little child within is still very much there, struggling on. If we want a struggle-free life, we need to reassure that little child and let them know that it's safe to let go. When they do, they get to play and have fun instead of worrying for us all the time. The 'adult us' can take over, living life through better relationships and mutual support, learning how to use creative solutions to challenges, and growing confident and wiser instead of being stuck in fear.

So these are the two things that can make it so hard to change: the influence of the subconscious, and the little child within. But these are not permanent blocks: we can change this. We can gently access the subconscious and we can reassure the little child within that it's OK to stop struggling. I've helped hundreds of people to do so already, through the tools and techniques of the Transformation Process.

The Transformation Process

All beliefs about struggle are based in fear — if we want to make room for love we need to clear these beliefs first.

Chapter Five
Introducing The Transformation Process

There are three parts to The Transformation Process, and it's important that you complete each part in order to get the full benefit. Have you ever eagerly rushed into some type of self-improvement activity and found you've given up because it doesn't seem to be working? Too often we try to jump ahead into the changes we want to make; we find a technique and think, **'I'll just do this and my whole life will change'** — but then it doesn't. So it's important to follow this process as it's presented.

Each part is tailored to not only bring about change but to clear the pathway for the next part to be successful.

The three parts of The Transformation Process are called:

» Part One: Trust in Surrender

» Part Two: Out of Fear

» Part Three: Into Love

I'm going to give you a summary of these below, and then I'll go on to explain each part in more depth in the following chapters. I'll also be teaching you some great methods and techniques to put the parts into practice.

Part One: Trust in Surrender

If we're going to let go of our beliefs about struggle, it's essential that we first acknowledge why these beliefs have played such an important role in our life. As we've seen, the little child within had a very good reason for forming those beliefs, so it's important not to deny them, push them away or see them as something wrong. These beliefs weren't wrong; they were perfectly appropriate for the time — they just don't work for us now in the adult world.

But as we've seen, the little child within finds it hard to let go of those unwanted beliefs, no matter how much we recognise that they're causing our struggles. This can be a huge obstacle when we want to make changes!

So in this first part of The Transformation Process, I'll be sharing with you a very powerful method to remedy this by helping the little child within to relinquish their need to struggle. It provides you with a way to let them know that you'll be finding ways of approaching life that are easier, more loving, and which don't require worrying, proving, and pleasing all the time. This part lays the groundwork to go on to the next parts of the process. **It is a hugely important step.** Skipping this is often the reason that people find it hard to start thinking and behaving differently, even though they desire to do so.

Part Two: Out of Fear

In Part Two of The Transformation Process, 'Out of Fear,' I'm going to share a powerful method to help clear those limiting beliefs. All beliefs about struggle are based in fear — if we want to make room for love we need to clear these beliefs first.

Anything that helps people recognise and begin to let go of unwanted beliefs is helpful — of course. However, traditional methods can take a great deal of homework and practice, and often only help a little towards belief changing. Many people report that later down the line, those thoughts and beliefs pop back up again, and they find that they're constantly trying to keep them at bay.

So in Part Two, I'll be showing you a powerful technique to help you gently get into the subconscious and clear those limiting beliefs permanently. It's called Emotional Freedom Techniques (EFT). An increasing number of therapists around the world are introducing EFT into their practice. In my experience, integrating EFT with traditional talk therapy models is very powerful for letting go of limiting beliefs and making space to create new and more helpful ways of approaching life. I've seen hundreds of people make rapid changes in their lives when they use this technique—and now you can too.

Part Three: Into Love—Bringing Love Back into Your Life

Part Three of The Transformation Process is all about tuning in and harnessing the power of love. Dr Wayne Dyer, author, speaker, teacher and an inspiration to millions of people around the world, said: 'When we are in fear there is no room for love, and when we are in love there is no room for fear.' This is so very apt for The Transformation Process. Parts One and Two of the process help you to let go of fear so that you can make room for love to flow more easily into your life. In Part Three, we'll be looking at just how powerful the energy of love can be; we'll be particularly focusing on loving ourselves. I'll be sharing practices which will help you to tune in and harness this magical energy in your life each and every day, and in particular those self-loving ways that the four struggle beliefs tend to make us forget.

The Transformation Process:

Part One

Trust in Surrender

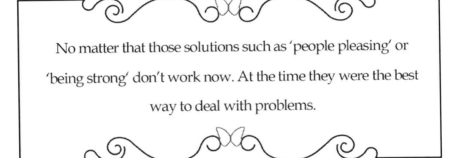

No matter that those solutions such as 'people pleasing' or 'being strong' don't work now. At the time they were the best way to deal with problems.

Chapter Six
A Very Important Friendship

'Tell your heart that the fear of suffering is worse than the suffering itself.
And that no heart has ever suffered when it goes in search of its dreams,
because every second of the search is a second's encounter with God and
with eternity.'

Paulo Coelho

As we've seen, in times of stress, it's often the little child within who's trying to run the show, but often people are not aware that this is happening. They feel in conflict a lot of the time because they try to make changes, and when they fail to do so, they get cross with themselves.

The problem is that when we become annoyed with ourselves for finding it hard to change, we're really getting annoyed with the little child within. It's their habit to earn and please their way into approval and acceptance from others. If we ourselves don't accept them, they're only going to feel even more compelled to carry on with this habit — this is why we become stuck.

So we need to start by acknowledging their existence and by making friends with them. We need to honour them for coming up with solutions that once enabled us to emotionally get by in the world, and thank them for their hard work.

It's also important to acknowledge that that little child will always be there — they're an integral part of us; they need to be reassured that, just because we're going to make changes, we won't be abandoning them. They need to trust that it's OK for them to let go of the struggle because we're going to take over and find ways of approaching life that are much easier. When we do this, the little child within can begin to relax and let the 'adult us' take over.

What follows is the first step towards letting go.

Writing a Very Important Letter

Setting the Scene

In many years of working with clients, I've found that one of the most powerful ways to connect with the little child within is to write them a letter. In this way we can honour them and thank them. Most importantly we can reassure them.

It's a good idea to take some time to set the scene before you do this exercise. I often suggest that people take a few days before they write their letter and that in quiet moments they think about the little boy or girl they once were. Here are some ideas to help you really tune in and connect with them. Not everyone is able to remember very much about their childhood; sometimes it's just a blur. If this is you, that's OK, but consider the following questions and see what comes to mind.

- » What did you look like as a small child?
- » Did you have long hair or short hair?
- » Were you on the tubby side or skinny, tall for your age, average or small?
- » What sort of clothes did you wear?
- » What sort of toys did you like to play with?
- » Did you have a nickname? If you did, think about your child self as this nickname; picture him or her in your mind's eye. If you didn't have a nickname just think of yourself as 'Little (your name).'
- » Dig out some old photos, if you have them, and spend some time looking into the eyes of your child self.

When you feel ready, find a private space where you have peace and time to write your letter. Write it in a way that feels right for you. Take some time over it and write as much or as little as you wish to, kindly and with love. Remember that the little child within is only young, so it's a good idea to speak to them in language that's appropriate for their age. Make sure you include the following:

Honour Them

First it's important to honour them — after all, when life was difficult they found solutions to help you survive hurts and rejections and to get people onside. No matter that those solutions such as 'people pleasing' or 'being strong' don't work now. At the time they were the best way to deal with problems.

So acknowledge and honour those solutions and the hard work your little child has put in to keep you safe over the years.

Thank Them

Next, let them know how much you value them; say, 'Thank you,' for their hard work, and tell them how grateful you are to them for their efforts in struggling for you. Remember, the little child within may well have had many messages that told them they were wrong or bad, so it's important to let them know that they have done nothing wrong and that you wholly accept them. By saying, 'Thank you,' you acknowledge that small child as essentially good, and you reassure them that they've been doing a great job in the best way they can.

Reassure Them

Finally, let them know that it's time for you, the adult, to take over and that you're finding easier ways to deal with life's problems; they can remove their suit of armour now; they don't need to battle on and be the hero anymore. Reassure them that you're not trying to get rid of them and that you will keep them safe in your heart-space always, but that they can start to have fun and be joyful now, instead of carrying the burden of your problems.

Writing this letter, connecting with the little child within — this can bring up a lot of emotions for you, so you may find it very helpful to have someone at hand to support you after you've written it. It's quite normal to cry and often these are tears of relief, so be gentle with yourself if you feel moved to tears.

Alongside writing this letter, some people also like to burn a candle as a ceremonial way of letting go of the past and inviting in the future. If this is something you would like to do: go ahead.

Amanda kindly offered to share her letter. Here is the beautiful letter she wrote:

Amanda's Letter

Dear Little Amanda,

All these years you've been there with me, helping me to survive in the world by wanting me to keep people happy and to please them so that I could feel safe and get them to like me. You've reminded me to be strong, to work extra hard so that people would be nice back; and that worked really well once upon a time. I just want to say Thank You so much for being there for me and trying to take care of me. I think you're an amazing and clever little girl for coming up with those ways to make life better.

When you decided, all those years ago, that keeping people happy was the right thing to do, it helped. But life has changed and, in fact, living life this way has been making me tired and unhappy for quite a while now. So it's time for us to do life differently. It's time to stop worrying about pleasing people. You don't have to go anywhere, you can stay here with me in my heart and I'll take care of you now. Nothing bad will happen—only good things— and we'll be very happy, and we can dance and play and be close with people, just like you did a long time ago before life got hard.

Now, it's time for me to take care of us both and I am going to do that by finding new ways of keeping us safe and happy. I'm getting some help from other grown-ups and I'm learning how to let the power of love come in and help us too. We don't have to just get by and survive in the world any more, Little Amanda, we can do it differently now; we can be really happy and have lots of fun together from now on.

Thank You, Little Amanda, for being there for me all this time. I will take it from here.

I love you.

You may want to read your letter out loud to a friend. Or you may both want to do this exercise and read your letters to each other.

Now that you've made contact with your little child within, remember that you can always speak with them, out loud or in your thoughts. It's a really good idea to have a chat with them from time to time, in quiet moments, when you're washing up perhaps, or maybe walking the dog.

They'll always be there with you, in your heart-space. It's good to tell them how much you love them, and to remind them about the things you've said in your letter. You'll be reinforcing those loving messages for them and they'll be happy to surrender their control and allow you to get on with the next job, which is clearing your unwanted beliefs. We'll be doing exactly this in Part Two of The Transformation Process, 'Clearing Away the Fear Clutter.'

The Transformation Process:

Part Two

Out of Fear

I see EFT as a technique that's been waiting for us all to catch up
with it — it's part of the magic of quantum understanding — the
evolutionary journey of mankind.

Chapter Seven
Clearing Away the Fear Clutter

'Your task is not to seek for love, but merely to seek and find all the barriers within yourself that you have built against it.'

Course in Miracles

When life's a struggle it can sometimes seem as though love isn't there at all. It *is* there, it's just that our way of approaching life becomes so cluttered up with fear that we can't find the space to let love in. This is why it's so important to make a start on clearing the fear that's causing blocks *before* we turn our attention to self-love practices. We don't have to clear it *all* out—that's an ongoing practice—but we do need to make a good start on decluttering fear so that love can flow in more easily.

An interesting image for this comes from the practice of Feng Shui, which suggests that we imagine a house with water flowing through it, identify the areas where that water would go stagnant, and then declutter those areas to allow the free flow of positive energy. That image provides an interesting parallel between our home and our subconscious mind. If our home is full of clutter, we feel stagnant and unhappy and so we need to declutter it to set things right again. When our subconscious is clogged up with *Fear Clutter* in the form of limiting beliefs about struggle, we also feel stuck and unhappy, so we need to declutter our subconscious and make way for new, healthier beliefs to form.

So How Do We Declutter the Subconscious?

Once we recognise that we have a limiting belief, the next step is to identify how that belief first came about. A good way to do this is to consider how certain experiences form beliefs. If we have a mundane experience that holds no particular meaning for us and has no emotional intensity, we're unlikely to form any beliefs around that experience. However, there are also experiences that:

» Are emotionally charged in some way

» Are troubling

» Make a deep impression

» Have an accompanying physical sensation, such as a pounding heart or churning stomach

» Require thinking of some way that would help make a situation better

These are the intense experiences that form our beliefs. It makes perfect sense then, that in order to let go of a belief, we need to recall those experiences and separate out the emotional intensity from those experiences. Once we do this, those experiences just become information in our mind; they have little meaning to us, and we're no longer compelled to run our lives according to their impact on us.

So how can we do this? How can we separate out the various aspects of an experience—the words, the messages, the images, the physical sensations, etc.? Until quite recently it's been difficult. Today, however, modern-day Energy Psychology techniques such as EFT enable us to do so.

EFT is Not About *Deleting* Memories from Your Mind

Let's be clear here: EFT is not about getting into your subconscious and deleting memories—that would be too strange! What EFT does do is help to clear away the emotional charge that's attached to those memories so that those experiences simply lose their power over you. It is aptly called Emotional Freedom Techniques because it frees you from the impact of troubling experiences.

What is Feeling Our Emotions?

As we saw in Chapter Three, 'How We Learnt To Struggle,' certain experiences have an impact on small children because their brain-waves vibrate at a specific frequency (4 Hz − 8 Hz) to allow them to absorb a lot of information from the external world. This is part of children's normal development process.

In EFT, any emotionally charged, negative experience can be seen as a trauma. Traumas can range from a small trauma, i.e. something as simple as a teacher giving a child a cross look, to a big trauma such as a car accident or an assault. Whether a trauma is big or small and whether it happens to us personally, to a loved one, or even if we witness it, we'll always feel some sort of emotion in response to it.

What does 'feeling an emotion' actually mean? To feel an emotion in response to an event describes a combination of two things: the thought we have about the event, and the physical sensations we experience at the time. For example, say something happens that makes us feel frightened; we may well have fearful thoughts such as 'Oh no!' accompanied by a pounding of our heart and catching our breath. That experience then, in the form of thoughts and physical sensations, gets locked into our subconscious.

Theo recalled a memory of one day in school, many years before. His teacher shouted at him:

> **'Theo! Why are you being so difficult today!'**

The teacher's words and tone of voice, his angry expression: all this sensory information became imprinted in Theo's subconscious. As Theo recalled this incident from such a long time ago, his heart pounded and his stomach churned.

Even though this was a memory of an event that happened over forty years previously, as I mentioned before, the subconscious doesn't know the difference between the past and the present. Therefore, it didn't take much more than recalling the event for the emotions that accompanied it to pop up to the surface of Theo's awareness. So how do we store all that information in our subconscious? And for that matter, where exactly is the subconscious?

EFT and the Body–Mind

Quantum physics tells us that our entire universe is made up of energy in its many forms, and so we too are beings of energy. Where traditionally the mind and body have been regarded as distinct and separate from one another, we now see them as a combined unit—a field of energy which we call the body–mind. And where traditionally the subconscious has been localised in the brain, more recently, we've come to understand that the subconscious is energetic information which is stored in the body–mind.

When we have an experience, we store away that information in the form of thoughts, images, physical sensations etc. in the subconscious, and when we recall those experiences, we recall the same energetic information. When we talk about accessing the subconscious then, we're talking about accessing that energetic information from the body–mind.

EFT is based on the principle that when our energy is flowing freely, we're happy and when it's blocked we're unhappy. When we have experiences that are negative, those unhappy thoughts, images and physical sensations can become locked in and cause a block, like a disruptive 'Zzzz' in the flow of our energy. We don't feel good and that's a sign that those blocks need to be released. You may recognise this from a time when you've had a good cry and felt much better afterwards. Perhaps you remember that you felt lighter and you sensed that something had shifted within you? This is because you released the blocked energy, what I've been calling 'fear clutter,' and you found the natural flow of you again. This is what EFT does, and it's so clever because it can find trapped emotional traumas from years ago, even decades earlier in life, and it helps to clear those blocks permanently.

EFT and Cognitive Shifts

EFT is often described as the interface between the conscious and subconscious, because not only does it find and release those trauma blocks, it also creates a calmer space for us to reframe our thoughts and to make a cognitive shift on what we've mistakenly believed to be true.

Cognitive shifts are the beginnings of belief changing; they are ways of thinking about an upsetting memory from a fresh perspective, usually more of an adult perspective. If you recall: when we feel stressed, it's because we're seeing the world through the eyes of the struggling child within. For example, when Theo used EFT to clear the emotional intensity from that memory of his teacher shouting at him, the emotional trauma of it, the block, was released. This provided him with space and clarity to reflect on that event as an adult. His cognitive shift was that he understood that maybe the teacher was simply having a bad day or been feeling unwell. And of course the more emotional blockages that Theo cleared, and the more cognitive shifts he had, the more his belief of *I Have to Prove Myself* faded away.

Like Theo, once you're able to detach from the traumatic impact of past memories, you'll find that those memories hold less meaning for you and so the beliefs around them will disappear. You'll start seeing life very differently; your relationships, work confidence — all of it will improve because you no longer see yourself in a certain way or think you have to be a certain way to get approval and love.

I've lost count of the number of lives I've seen transformed by clearing past traumas and unwanted beliefs with EFT. As a therapist, I see EFT as a technique that's been waiting for us all to catch up with it — it's part of the magic of quantum understanding — the evolutionary journey of mankind. In the next chapter I'm going to teach you how to apply EFT as a regular practice.

It occurred to me that whilst the idea of actually tapping on our body may seem like a new concept, it's actually a natural thing for us to tap.

Chapter Eight

Practising Emotional Freedom Techniques

'The cause of all negative emotions is a disruption in the body's energy system.'

Gary Craig

EFT is similar to modern-day acupuncture in that it uses the energy system called meridians to access and redirect our energy, and to discharge unwanted blocks in the energy flow. Unlike acupuncture, with EFT there are no needles, and instead we use our fingers to lightly tap on specific acupuncture points on the body. People are often stunned at how quickly they feel a release of blocked emotions. When we stop to consider that the original trauma which caused the blockage probably only lasted moments, if not seconds, it makes sense that it would just take a very short time to let it go. Once we know how.

We've All Been Tapping for a Very Long Time!

When I first started using EFT with my clients, I was amazed at how quickly they picked it up. It's a relatively simple process, but I noticed that clients seemed to almost *know* the points. It occurred to me that whilst the idea of actually tapping on our body may seem like a new concept, it's actually a natural thing for us to tap. Think of a crying baby: we pick them up in our arms and we gently tap on their back to soothe them. Think about a time when you were unhappy and upset: did someone tap your knee or arm to comfort you? And we even pat our dogs—which incidentally is the word *tap* back to front!

Before We Begin: Some Very Important Points

Upset or Tearful

Just before I teach you the EFT tapping procedure, I want to share a couple of important points with you. Firstly, it's very important to be aware of the power of your memories. One of the reasons both therapists and their clients enjoy using EFT so much is that it works so rapidly. There's no need for many weeks of chewing over and over why something has been such a big problem and trying to let it go through sheer willpower. With EFT you simply identify a memory linked to the issue that's troubling you, and then clear the associated emotional intensity from that memory. Quite often, as you clear the intensity from one memory, another memory pops up to the surface for you to clear away. On rare occasions, a very distressing memory may pop up—perhaps something you haven't thought about in a long time, or had not even remembered before at all. This can make you feel upset or tearful.

Should this happen, it's very important that you continue to tap, even if you feel very upset and emotional. Remember, it's the emotional blockage that's coming to the surface, and as you keep tapping, so you release that distress from your system once and for all.

If you think you may have some very deep and distressing issues to work on, I recommend you skip the following sections on EFT and seek a professional EFT practitioner, such as myself or another qualified therapist, for some sessions. These sessions can be done in person or online. You can find my details and more information in 'Resources' in this book.

It can also be helpful to practice EFT with a friend, taking it in turn to talk about your issues, recalling specific events that you wish to tap on, and supporting each other if either of you feel the need.

Feeling Tired

Have you ever had a huge, long cry over something and then afterwards felt better, but really tired? With EFT you may or may not cry, but because you're releasing a lot of emotional intensity which may have been held in your system for a long time, there's a similar feeling of relief and you may well feel tired for a while afterwards, or even the next day. As you begin to practice EFT on a regular basis, this feeling of tiredness will lessen and, after a while, you'll begin to feel more energised than ever!

Put Away Your Mobile

When you practice EFT, you're going to be working with your energy fields, so it's a good idea to put away anything that may interfere with that, such as mobile phones or any other magnetic items. Staying hydrated is also a big help, so be sure to drink plenty of fluids.

Now I'm going to explain how we practice the technique of EFT (*this is also shown on the bonus videos on the book website*)

> » First I am going to help you identify a memory to work with.
> » Then I'm going to show you the tapping points.
> » Then I'll describe the technique of tapping on those points.

Here's the EFT process, step by step.

Step 1: Identify the Issue to Work On

Step 2: Rate the Initial Intensity

Step 3: Create the Set-up Statement

Step 4: Create the Reminder Phrase

Step 5: Check the Intensity

Step 1: Identify the Issue to Work On

EFT can be used to address any number of issues. In this case, we're going to be addressing those four beliefs about struggle (actually they account for many of the problems we have in life). So to begin, I'm going to ask you to recall a time when something happened: the memory of an event which led to one of these beliefs. Just as a reminder, these four beliefs are:

> » I Must Be Strong
> » I Have To Please People
> » I Need To Prove Myself
> » I Have To Do Everything By Myself

I've suggested throughout this book that you jot down any memories that came up for you during your reading. It's at this point that they come in handy! Look through your writings and see what memory you can use. If you haven't got notes, that's OK. I've included a handy exercise below to help you get started.

When you decide on a memory to work with, try to make it as specific as possible. For example:

'When I was ten, I was scared when Mum shouted at me for breaking the milk jug' is much more specific than:

'When I was ten, I was upset because Mum was angry.'

To give you an idea, here are some of the events that Theo identified for his own EFT practice. He was working on clearing the belief 'I Need To Prove Myself'.

» When I was six, my mother said I was a mistake and I was really hurt.

» Dad shouted and sent me to my room when I spilt milk on the carpet.

» My eighth birthday party was cancelled and all my classmates teased me.

As you can see, these memories all come from Theo's childhood. It's helpful to remember that our more recent experiences don't actually *create* our beliefs — they just reinforce the beliefs we formed earlier in life. It's a good idea, then, to try to focus on the earliest memories you can think of, and this way, the impact of experiences that came later will simply fade away by themselves.

Identify a Memory Worksheet

Sometimes we can easily remember childhood events. However, it's not unusual to look back at the past and it looks like one big blur and nothing very specific comes to mind. If you can't remember all the way back to events in your childhood, that's perfectly OK; just go back to a more recent event and start from there. Once you start your EFT tapping practice you'll find that more memories from earlier and earlier events will pop up for you — it's like clearing a pathway back through time.

A good way to get used to working with EFT is to talk with a friend (or imagine talking with a friend) about some recent event that has bothered you. (Bear in mind that if it's something that's bothered you, it's very likely tied in with one of your beliefs: otherwise it wouldn't bother you so much!) Perhaps it is something to do with work, or with another friend or a family member. Perhaps it concerns an argument with your partner or something that happened with a project you've been working on. Tune in to that memory: maybe you can picture it in your mind's eye, or maybe you just have a strong sense of how it felt. Notice the emotional feeling that the memory brings to you. Some examples are anger, panic, despair, insecurity, and a sense of being overwhelmed.

Notice the physical sensations in your body. Examples of this can be pounding of the heart, churning of the stomach and tightness in throat.

Fill in the following:

When _____ happened:

I felt _____

And in my body I could feel _____

And I thought _____

And now I come to think about it, I see that it fits in with the belief that _____ (<u>Choose one of the Four Struggle Beliefs</u>)

> » I must be strong
> » I need to please people
> » I have to prove myself
> » I have to do everything by myself

> Your memory may apply to more than one of these
>
> beliefs — that's OK, they all have struggle in common. Just
>
> choose one that feels right in the moment.

You can choose to work with this memory now, or if you prefer to, go back further in time, ask yourself the following questions and see what pops up for you.

> » When was the last time I felt like this?
> » Is there an earlier time in my life when I felt this way?
> » When is the *earliest* time in my life I felt like this?

If something pops up from an earlier time then great, you can work on that early memory.

If it's something from childhood, remember to *tune in to your inner child*, just as you did in the first part of The Transformation Process, when you connected with them through your letter.

However, if you only have a recent event to work on, that's absolutely fine. You'll find that as you clear the more current events, memories from further back will rise to the surface of your awareness. Just remember to only ever work on one memory at a time in your EFT practice.

You have now identified:

» A memory of an event that is associated with one of the four beliefs about struggle

» The emotions (including physical) that go with that particular memory

Step 2: Rate the Initial Intensity

Now that you have the memory, the next step is to take a measure. What's the emotional intensity you feel when you tune in to that memory? Give it a rating from 1 to 10, where:

1 = I'm not really bothered by it.

10 = It's very bad indeed.

Step 3: Create the Set-up Statement

We now have a memory and a rating of its intensity; the next step is to create a set-up statement. We use the set-up to begin a session of EFT tapping. The set-up statement goes as follows:

'**Even though** (*insert the memory you've identified and how you feel about it*), **I deeply and completely love and accept myself.'**

For example, Theo wanted to let go of his need to prove himself. He identified a memory: the time when his mother told him he was a mistake and he'd felt so anxious. So his set-up statement was:

'**Even though when I was six, Mum said I was a mistake and I felt so anxious, I deeply and completely love and accept myself.'**

(If you don't feel comfortable saying I deeply and completely love and accept myself — choose a phrase such as I'm working on loving and accepting myself.)

For the set-up statement, you tap on the Karate Chop (KC) Point.

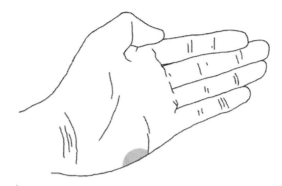

'**Even though** (memory and how you feel about it), **I deeply and completely love and accept myself.**'

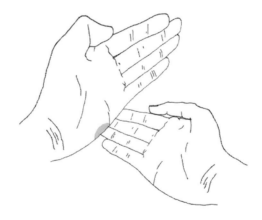

With the fingers of your other hand, tap gently about 7 times on your KC point and repeat your set-up statement.

This step covers two important points.

1. It helps focus your subconscious on what issue you wish to clear.

2. It offers self-acceptance, which is the most important starting point for any transformation to take place. Remember in Part One of The Transformation Process you reassured the little child within that you'll be taking over now? When you're using the set-up statement, it's you the adult who is taking over and using the technique to help the little child within to let go of their traumas, limiting beliefs, and their fears.

The simple act of declaring 'Even though I have this problem I love and accept myself' is you the grown-up telling the little child within that a problem is 'just a problem'; it's not bigger than you, you're ready and able to let it go. And not only this, but you're harnessing the power of love to help you do so!

Step 4: The Reminder Phrase

This step focuses on the emotions, including the physical ones, associated with that memory as you tune in to it.

For example, when Theo thought about his mum saying he was a mistake, he felt anxious and his stomach churned. So his reminder phrase was:

'All this anxiety in my stomach.'

Examples of your reminder phrase could be:

'All this hurt in my heart'

'All this anxiety in my throat'

'All this anger in my stomach'

'All this frustration in my shoulders'

'All this overwhelm in my chest'

Start tapping on the points in the order shown below. Start from the top of your head and work down. Tap each point about 7 times, repeating your reminder phrase.

Continuing on with Theo as our example: he started at the top of his head (TH) tapping about 7 times, saying 'All this anxiety in my stomach.' He continued on through each point repeating this statement.

Simply repeat your reminder phrase as you tap on each point. When you have finished tapping on the last point, take a deep breath.

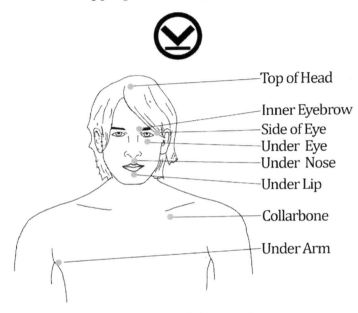

TH – Top of the Head

IE – Inner Eyebrow

SE – Side of Eye

UE – Under the Eye

UN – Under Nose

UL – Under Lip

CB – Collarbone

UA – Under Arm

Step 5: Rate the Intensity Again

Keep tapping round the points until you feel a shift in the intensity of your emotions. When you feel ready, review your progress. Think about that memory, really focus on it and compare it against your 1–10 rating from Step 2. It will very likely be reduced to a zero or be very low. If you feel it's still too high, keep tapping until it decreases.

At the end of a round, you may find that your emotions have changed. For example, 'overwhelm in my chest' has lessened, but now your emotions have moved to 'anger in my stomach.' That's OK—this is perfectly normal. Go through the tapping points again in the same way as before, but repeat the new reminder phrase. For example, 'this anger in my stomach.'

Look out for cognitive shifts, such as 'It's over; it's just something that happened; I'm safe, I can't feel it anymore; I can let it go now, it seems less important now; I see things differently.'

Making a cognitive shift about an event doesn't mean denying the event ever happened. It just means seeing it in a more helpful, more adult and less emotionally distressing way.

Just before we go on, here are some common questions about the actual technique of tapping.

EFT Frequently Asked Questions

Do I tap on my left or my right side?

You can tap on either side.

Can I switch sides in the middle of tapping through the points?

Yes, you can.

How many times do I tap on each point?

You tap approximately seven times on each point.

How many fingers do I tap with?

Tap with two or more fingertips.

I Feel Worse When I Start

Occasionally you may notice that you feel a little worse when you start tapping. It's because you are focusing on the problem and therefore an emotion is coming to the surface. Just keep tapping and you'll be able to let it go.

Why Does EFT Focus on the Negative?

In recent times there has been increasing awareness of the benefits of focusing on the positive aspects of life. A common question about EFT therefore is 'Why do we focus on the negative?' EFT Founder Gary Craig says:

'The language that we use always aims at the negative. This is essential because we want to bring up the negative emotion, which is often buried deeply, and clear it away. By contrast, conventional methods and popular self-help books encourage positive thinking and suggest avoiding the negative. This sounds good but, for our purposes, it does little more than cover over the negative with pleasant-sounding words, a bit like papering over the cracks in a wall. EFT, on the other hand, aims at the negative so that it can be cleared out once and for all. This allows our natural positives to bubble up to the top.'

I agree and, as I've been describing for The Transformation Process, this is what we've been doing here in Part Two: clearing away the 'fear clutter' so that we make it easier for creativity and inspiration, connectedness and wisdom, and love to bubble up!

An Ongoing Practice

EFT works best as an ongoing practice; it's good to make it make it a part of your daily routine. As you do so, you'll notice you will feel happier and happier, because every time you work on a memory, you'll dismantle your limiting beliefs a little more. You'll be surprised how quickly you'll see changes in how you think, and feel, and behave. Those parts of your life that have been problematic and a struggle become much easier, and you'll find you feel more inspired for the future.

I know that I couldn't help people to the level that I do if I hadn't cleared away my own limiting beliefs and created new, more helpful ones. Today, whilst I'm not the struggler I once was, I still have challenging times; occasionally the last vestiges of an old belief about needing to prove myself or be strong in some way pops up. And when I recognise this, I track back to a memory and tap to clear the impact of that. With EFT, we can radically change how we approach life — living life from a perspective of fear becomes a thing of the past as we make more room for love.

As you read and complete the practices in the following chapters, you may remember more past experiences that have contributed to your beliefs about struggle. It's a good idea to add them to your notebook for future EFT sessions.

The Transformation Process:

Part Three

Into Love

As small children we were dependent on others to show us

these loving ways; as adults we can choose to bring these

self-loving ways into our lives for ourselves.

Chapter Nine
Into Love: The Power

'I am the universe
The universe is me
I am all-powerful
I am free.'
Marléne Rose Shaw

Have you ever looked at images of our home, planet Earth, and been blown away by the beauty of it all? The abundance of blue water, the awe-inspiring land masses, the polar caps. And that luminous haze of blue which embraces and protects us all—it's breath-taking.

I think there's something quite poignant, and a little comical, about the fact that so many of us are running around stressed, feeling so alone and worrying about not being loved enough, when all the time the evidence of how much we're loved is right under our noses! It's obvious from the fact that we have our beautiful home planet Earth. It's obvious in sunlight, air, water, and plants. It's obvious in the existence of life itself.

Two things we can be certain of: life will always seek to expand into more life in some form, and life always knows what it's doing. Think about a baby developing in the womb: how do the cells know to form arms and legs and a face, and where to put them? Or a seed—it doesn't look anything like a flower, but we know that if we plant it, it will in fact grow into a flower.

There are never any strings attached to the process of life—the sun doesn't have to struggle to rise each day, plants don't have to earn their right to grow, and birds don't need to prove they can fly! All of life works in harmony; every living being is part of a system, connected by a creative and intelligent power. But what is this power?

Human beings have always asked such questions because we're so inquisitive; that's one of the reasons we've evolved as a race — our nosiness! It's this curiosity about ourselves and our world that has led to the great advances in our sciences. And as I mentioned before, today we've come to understand our world in quantum terms; we view our world now and everything within it as energy. This has brought a whole new way of viewing life.

The Matrix of all Matter

The father of quantum physics, Max Planck, said:

All matter originates and exists only by virtue of a force which brings the particle of an atom to vibration and holds this most minute solar system of the atom together. We must assume behind this force the existence of a conscious and intelligent mind. This mind is the matrix of all matter.

It's through our understanding of quantum physics that we've more fully embraced the interconnectedness of life. Prior to this, science saw the world as a vast collection of separate entities; these entities — planets, objects, people, even the mind and the body — all co-existed, yet were completely distinct from each other. In the quantum way of understanding our universe, we see that, instead of existing separately, everything exists 'in relationship' within a constant dynamic exchange of energy.

I had a profound experience of this interconnectedness when I was nineteen years old. I was on a coach travelling from London to visit my family on the south coast; it was a summer evening, around 6 p.m. As the coach drove past a large hillside, I suddenly had the most peculiar feeling — it was as though I had grown into a huge child, fifty feet tall, and I was playfully rolling down that hill. Yet not just down it, but through it! It was as if I, and all the land around me, had merged into one. I felt that I was part of some greater intelligent power: myself, the hill, and the entire universe connected as one. This experience came out of nowhere and disappeared after some moments, but in that time I felt a sense of well-being that is hard to put into words. It was a type of absolute happiness, as though all was well, all was love and I was loved; I saw the wisdom of the universe, the creation and interconnectedness of everything and I was completely supported by a loving intelligence — and I felt peaceful. Since then, I've discovered that many people across the world report such peak experiences.

Today, several decades later, I often tune in and ask that loving intelligence to help me in my therapy practice. Qualifications, training, and years of experience have provided me with fantastic tools to help my clients. However, when I put my trust in that loving power, there's something more going on; something magical comes into the therapy room. I only have to quietly ask and I'm given access to intuitive information: images, ideas, thoughts, sensations, and 'knowings' just seem to pop into my mind. It's a wonderful sense of connectedness, of tuning in with a loving, creative energy which is providing me with the information I need to help my client move forward and find the wisdom that makes their life easier, and happier.

People have different names for this loving intelligence: The Creator, The Divine, Source and many more. It really doesn't matter what words we use — the heart of this powerful intelligence is the same, regardless of the words we use. I like to use the word 'Love,' because 'Love' is a word that describes both the essence of this miraculous power *and* the experience of being connected with it. We can always tell when we're tuned in to this magical power because we feel happy and at ease with life. It's the power of love that gives us that great feeling of connectedness in our relationships. It's the power of love that makes life effortless by offering us inspiration and creative solutions so that we can grow and evolve into our happy life.

If we've grown up believing that we can be separated from love, it can be hard to take on-board that love will be there for us without having to struggle to earn it in some way. But actually, there's nothing we have to do to bring it into our lives except to remember it exists.

We need only understand that the infinite power of love is unconditional; it doesn't expect anything from us, ever. It doesn't require us to prove ourselves to get its attention, it doesn't ask that we please it in some way; it doesn't expect us to endure hardships and struggle through life alone. It only ever sees each and every one of us as one hundred per cent worthy. And it is *always* there: it always has been and it always will be.

Just Ask Love

Amanda arrived at one of our sessions literally beaming.

'It works!' she said.

'What's that?' I smiled back.

'What you said last week: when you don't know what to do ... just ask love!'

So how do we just ask love? How do we open the door to let love flow into our lives, in particular if we've been so used to struggling alone? It may seem that love is out of our reach. However, it's very simple. All that's required of us is to remember to place our focus on it. It's so much easier than we realise because we've been so cluttered up with fear that we haven't had room to notice love in our lives.

The more we clear fear from our lives, the easier it becomes to place our attention on love. In Parts One and Two of The Transformation Process we cleared the pathway and made room for love. All we need do now is begin to focus and to think and to behave in self-loving ways.

Reversing the Cycle: Out of Fear, Into Love

In Chapter Two, 'Why is My Life Such a Struggle?' we saw that for each of the four struggle beliefs there's a corresponding type of self-love that gets forgotten. We saw how this creates a cycle: Fear — Forgotten Self-love — More Fear.

Believing we must be strong means we forget to be kind to ourselves.

Believing we have to please people means we forget to focus on our own worth.

Believing we need to prove ourselves means we forget to accept ourselves as we are.

Believing we have to do everything alone means we forget to seek out and trust in the support of others.

What better way is there to reverse this cycle, to move further out of fear and into love, than consciously practising these forgotten self-loving ways? As small children we were dependent on others to teach us about kindness, self-worth and acceptance, and trust; as adults we can choose to gift ourselves with these loving ways. We so often think about these ways of being in general terms, we get that they're a good idea, but I can tell you that they are oh so much more powerful than simply that! These ways of being are the ingredients of love's magic, and when we choose to use them, the power of love reorganises the entire universe in helpful and creative ways for us. The most miraculous things begin to occur: connections happen as the right people show up and opportunities appear as if out of nowhere. I've lost count of the number of times I've seen people's lives transformed as they start practising these self-loving ways. In the next chapter we're going to make a start with self-kindness.

If that power can sustain the entire universe, it's much more potent and dependable than any strength we try to summon up by enduring hardships.

Chapter Ten

Into Love: The Power in Self-Kindness

'Develop the strength to do bold things, not the strength to suffer.'
Niccolò Machiavelli

Whenever I ask someone, 'Are you kind?' they most often say, 'Yes, of course!'

Yet when I follow that with, 'And are you kind to yourself?' they have to pause for a moment to think, and quite often they tell me they're not even sure what that would feel like.

How do you answer the question 'Are you kind to yourself?'

Whatever your answer is, I'm sure you'll agree that we can all benefit from being kinder to ourselves — but when we believe 'I have to be strong,' self-kindness is left by the wayside because we're so busy firefighting problems that we simply forget. It's as though we're wearing 'self-kindness blinkers'; we don't see that there's a bigger picture behind the challenging situations that come up in life, and we don't consider if there may be less harsh and more loving ways to approach those situations.

Self-kindness brings *Real* Strength

If we've spent our whole lives struggling, it's easy to think that that's what strength is all about— enduring hardship in the face of difficulty. But that's not real strength: it's suffering. It keeps us stuck in our problems instead of helping us grow and move forward in life. Yet, from the very moment we even consider how we can be kinder to ourselves, we connect with an infallible strength. It's the strength that comes from the power of love — if that power can sustain the entire universe then it's much more potent and dependable than any strength we try to summon up through enduring hardships.

Self-kindness is actually a form of gratitude; it's saying 'I acknowledge the gift of my life and I'm doing that by appreciating myself and treating myself in more loving ways.'

And as we get into the habit of listening in to our feelings and treating ourselves with loving care, so our relationships with others become more loving; more secure and more supportive. No longer feeling driven to endure hardships, we have fewer things to cope and struggle with, and that provides more space and time for creative energy to flow into our lives. It all becomes so much easier.

But Am I Being Selfish?

One of the misconceptions I've heard from people over the years is that it's somehow selfish to love yourself. It's understandable that people can think this way given that for generations we've been passing on the mistaken idea that there's not enough love to go round.

Actually, it's just the opposite. The more we love ourselves, the more we bring that loving energy into our lives and thus the more we have to give. One great way to help ourselves embrace self-kindness is to remember that each and every time we think a kind thought about ourselves, we're helping to break the chain of generations of unkind thoughts and criticisms. Being kind to our own self is being kind to the future of all human kind — self-kindness, then, is a win-win situation!

Self-kindness is good for our health too. Research has shown that kindness increases the health and wellbeing of the person who is receiving the kindness, as well as the person who is offering kindness and anyone who is observing the kind act! That's compelling evidence of the power of love working its magic. If you want to find out more on this subject, I recommend you read *Why Kindness is Good For You* by David R. Hamilton, PhD.

Grace
Removing the Self-Kindness Blinkers

As far back as Grace could remember, she'd thought that life was all about gritting her teeth and just getting on with whatever was thrown at her. She'd never stopped to think about self-kindness as a 'thing' in her life — something she could actually put into practice. Grace didn't blame her mother for the problems of her childhood; as an adult herself, she now realised how powerless and vulnerable her mother must have felt at the time.

In her EFT practice, Grace was able to clear the impact of those childhood experiences that had led her to believe she had to be strong all the time. Now it was time to bring more love into her life by focusing on being much kinder to herself. As Grace considered this simple notion, she told me she felt a tangible shift within herself.

She said:

> 'When I started thinking about being kind to myself, about loving myself, it was as if a warm blanket was wrapped around me and I realised that that was what I'd been trying to do with my addictions all along — to make myself feel better, to feel loved. It's amazing, just thinking about being kind to me... I don't feel so alone anymore.

Grace's description of a 'warm blanket' was very apt. When we bring self-kindness into our lives we create a wonderful field of 'kindness energy' around us; it's as though we're sending out the message:

'I'm being kind to myself because this is what I want in my life, and this is what I deserve.'

And so the power of love begins to rearrange the entire universe in our favour, and it gives us that same kindness back, in bundles!

Grace started to speak to herself in more loving ways instead of mentally beating herself up. She also started to consider what she wanted out of life. She decided that instead of drifting from one unwanted hardship to another, she would begin to actively create her life as she wanted it to be. And as she started to focus on being kinder to herself in these ways, Grace just happened to see an ad for a new yoga class and felt confident enough to take it up. At the class, she met a new friend who invited her to join a ramblers' group. There, she met more new friends who treated themselves with kindness too! Grace was happier than she had ever thought possible.

Three Practices in Self-Kindness

Because I'm Being Kind

In my experience, people often feel a bit bewildered and are unsure where to start with self-kindness. It's not unusual for people to say, 'Where do I start? How do I do it?' And even... 'Is this another thing I'm going to get wrong?'

One powerful and yet very simple self-kindness exercise, which I've used to help many people over the years, is called 'Because I'm Being Kind.' This exercise involves focusing on the self-kindness you're *already* practising in your life. It's a great way to bring self-kindness in, because it takes away any apprehension about having to start something new, or 'getting it right.' You're already doing it and you've already been getting it right—all you need to do now is notice it.

These little *noticings* work like magic—I've had many, many people over the years tell me they're amazed at the feeling of loving energy that comes over them as they pay attention to them. Here are some suggestions to get you started.

When you brush your teeth, look into the mirror and purposefully say to yourself:

'I'm brushing my teeth because I know they're worth looking after. I'm doing this because I'm being kind to myself and I'm worth loving.'

After you've cooked a meal and you're eating it, think to yourself:

'I'm feeding myself this lovely meal because I know I'm worth looking after — I'm doing this because I'm being kind to myself and I'm loveable.'

As you go to bed at night, think to yourself:

'I'm getting some rest now because I know that it's a good idea to be healthy and I'm being kind to myself, because that's how I want to live my life.'

These suggestions may seem almost too simple — yet so often our heads are filled with thoughts on what's going wrong and how unhappy we are with ourselves. By focusing on these small acts of self-kindness, we're tuning in to the support of love's power. It's always there for us; there's really no need to worry and fret as we tend to do. And as we keep focusing on these small acts, this loving energy expands more, and more, and more, as new ideas for self-kindness present themselves to us.

The Stress-Ease Bucket

Having to be strong all the time increases stress levels. It's so easy to forget that it's possible to choose kindness instead. Using the 'Stress-Ease Bucket' image is a good way to remind yourself to focus on how kind you're being to yourself, or not, as it may be.

Start by imagining a bucket. Your bucket can be filled up with stress. Your bucket can also be emptied of stress by a tap attached to the side of it.

Consider that your EFT practice is the tap which releases stress from your bucket. As we've seen, EFT is a fantastic technique to help release the stress of traumatic experiences, both past and present.

But the question is 'What are you putting *into* your bucket today?' Whilst it's great to use EFT to release stress, we're not being kind to ourselves if we just continue filling up our bucket with more!

The Stress-Ease Bucket

Choices such as poor diet, overwork, not taking enough exercise and all the other unhelpful decisions we make each day: these are habits of being unkind to ourselves that we can fall into because we're not paying enough attention.

So it's always a good idea to ask yourself:

'What am I putting into my bucket today?'

If you become aware that you're filling up your bucket with less than kind thoughts and behaviours, here are some suggestions:

» Take a break: focus on a good balance of work and play.

» Be more aware of the food you're consuming, and the way you're eating it—slow down.

» Take some exercise. Between 15–30 minutes is good.

» Do some yoga, meditation, or some creative pursuit that you enjoy.

» Connect with a friend or family member just for the sake of it.

» What else can you put into your bucket that is kind to you?

Thinking from Your Inner Adult

Now that you're bringing self-kindness into your awareness, you may start to notice just how harshly you've been speaking to yourself. It's not helpful to have an inner dialogue consisting of self-criticism and disapproval (that's those old childhood messages).

Of course there are great benefits in talking to yourself in more kind and loving ways. But do be careful, because there's a common setback that often happens when people realise they've been mentally beating themselves up: they get into a pattern of overcompensating to the point that they keep themselves in struggle mode.

Some overcompensating thoughts are:

'I'm doing a great job despite all this difficulty!'

'Considering how hard this is, I'm managing very well!'

These types of thoughts may soothe your inner child for a while, but they tend to reinforce your *need to be strong in the face of adversity*, because they still focus on hardship. Instead, empower your inner child to join in with your inner adult with thoughts like:

'That's great; well done to me; I knew I could do it!'

'Is there another way I could approach this that would be kinder to myself?'

Do you see the subtle difference? When you make this small correction to your thinking, you'll start seeing your life as easier, much more empowered, and confident, rather than a struggle you have to overcome.

The problem is that if we're driven to please others, we put so much energy into earning their approval that we miss the point of our own worth!

Chapter Eleven
Into Love: The Power in Self-Worth

'In my room I have a mirror, and I call it My Magic Mirror.
Inside this mirror is my very best friend.'
Louise Hay

I've met a lot of people over the years who've asked me, 'Why don't other people treat me as well as I treat them?' I think it's true to say that all of us have had the experience of being disregarded at some point. I'm sure you'll agree that it's a very unpleasant feeling. But the majority of us are basically kind and caring people — in most cases, as I've mentioned before, the person doing the disregarding probably doesn't even register what they've done. They haven't intentionally set out to disrespect us; they just go by the signals we're giving out.

The problem is that if we're driven to please others, we put so much energy into earning their approval that we miss the point of our own worth! We forget to pay attention to ourselves and to value ourselves.

The worth that we can discover within us is solid and lasting and loving. Validation from others is transient and often dependent on their own current state of well-being. And much as we often wish they would recognise us for the valuable being that we are, the truth is that they only tend to see it when we ourselves see it.

Remembering Self-Worth → No Longer a Need To Please → Respect and Regard / Reciprocity / Personal space → Connectedness / Creativity / Wisdom / Happiness

When we pay attention to our own worthiness, we make a profound connection with the power of love that first brought us into this life. It's a way of saying thank you: 'Thank you, thank you for this life — see I'm treasuring it!' And by connecting with ourselves in this loving way, our connections with others improve because those relationships become all about respect and regard too.

Amanda
Wisdom in Taking Responsibility

Amanda came to see that she'd spent a great deal of her emotional energy focusing on how other people treated her. As she'd declared in our first session, 'They're treating me like dirt!' In her EFT practice she began to let go of the mistaken belief that keeping people happy was a good idea. She began making room in her life to start focusing on her own worth and her own needs; she recognised that by not making her own needs clear to others she held some responsibility for those bad experiences. I had to admire Amanda for her courage and growing wisdom as she acknowledged the part she'd played. It's not easy for us to do this — it's often so much easier to blame other people when they treat us poorly!

Amanda began to think about how she could make herself clearer to people, and what boundaries she could put in place. How could she let people know it was time to start respecting and regarding her as a valued friend, a respected family member, and a worthy person?

Knocking at the Front Door

Setting clear boundaries is so important in cherishing our own worth and asking the same from others. We already live in a world of boundaries and we manage these appropriately because we know that doing so will keep us safe and happy. Say, for example, someone wants to come into your home — you expect them to ring or knock at the door to announce their presence, so that you can decide if you wish to allow them in. You wouldn't welcome someone into your personal space who is abusive or disrespectful to you. Yet when it comes to our relationships, we often leave the door wide open! We make the mistake of thinking that people will automatically respect our boundaries when we ourselves aren't even sure of what those boundaries are. It's a bit like being so busy trying to fend off the people coming through the doorway that we haven't the time to stop and consider putting an actual door in place! This is what setting personal boundaries basically does: it reminds people, and ourselves, that we're of value.

I'm going to be sharing with you some practices that will help you set boundaries that will make a big difference to your confidence and your feeling of worthiness. These practices have been of immense benefit to many clients over the years. I use them in my own life too with great effect. Before we look at them though, I just want to mention a few things that might come up for you when you think about boundaries.

Ruffling Feathers

One of the common concerns that people express to me is the worry that the people they've been 'pleasing' will become angry or reject them if they suddenly start putting their own needs first. It's certainly true that when we first start putting ourselves first, some people may find it strange and even be a little put out. But it's important to bear with it. For a short time, it may seem like people's feathers are being ruffled, but these uncomfortable transitions often right themselves surprisingly quickly. The reason the shift is rapid is because when we begin to focus on our self-worth, we create a wonderful field of 'worthiness energy' around us which attracts more and more worthiness into our life. The intelligent and magical power of love only ever has our best interests at heart; it will shift worlds, and people, to make us happy.

A Quick Word on Barriers

Before we go on to the self-worth practices, I just want to make a quick distinction between boundaries and barriers. People sometimes think they are one and the same, but they're quite different, so it's a good idea to be clear.

Boundaries are created from self-respect, healthy relationships, a sense of worthiness, and love. Barriers are created from a place of fear and separation. People use barriers in order to protect themselves when they feel defenceless. They can appear cold and unfriendly when they're actually just trying to shield themselves from a situation in which they feel overwhelmed. It's always the struggling little child within that puts up barriers. You can recognise this in yourself or others when you or they:

» Withhold affection

» Say 'No' without explanation

» Withdraw

» Become angry and defensive

» Appear to be arrogant

On the other hand, when we set loving boundaries, we're coming from our adult self and we:

» Offer care and understanding

» Say 'No' with appropriate explanation

» Stay in communication (in the way that feels right)

» Remain calm

» Make agreements and find common ground

Four Practices in Self-Worth

The Daily Self-Worth Question

Each evening, for a week, think of the most challenging situation you had that day. Write the following in your notebook, filling in the details:

Today when (*the challenging situation*) happened, I thought _____ and I felt _____.

Then write this question:

How could I have thought about and approached (*the challenging situation*) in ways that value my worth?

You may have an answer straight away, or you may have to ponder it for a while, but it will come to you, and when it does, be sure to write it down. Doing so will set it firmly in your mind and you'll begin to feel stronger and more confident in yourself.

The *Don't Want—Do Want* Worksheet

When we spend a lot of time trying to keep other people happy, we can easily get overwhelmed with trying to do too many things at once. Trying to please everyone leads to pleasing no one and that just adds to the stress. Somewhere in the middle of all that, we lose ourselves, and life begins to feel out of our control. Does that sound familiar to you? I know I've been in that situation myself.

So what we really want is to be calm so that we can make space for love's creative energy to come into our lives and give us inspiring solutions to challenges.

As we've seen, one of the most effective ways to create clarity and bring self-worth into our lives is through setting appropriate boundaries. There can be a problem though: if we're feeling angry, resentful, and stuck, it can be hard to think clearly about what changes we want to make and how to communicate that to the people who are over-whelming us.

It's only natural, if we feel we're being treated poorly, to focus on what we don't want. For example, when someone disrespects us, it's so easy to think:

'I wish they wouldn't take me granted,' 'Why do they treat me like dirt?' 'They're never there for me,' and so on.

Notice these *don't want* words are all about disconnection in some form; they push us further away from love, and from each other. So instead of coming from a place of fear and disconnection, we need to put our focus on love and connection. It's very helpful indeed then to start thinking about what we *do want*. When we focus on letting people know what we *do want*, what we would like, we're connecting with them rather than pushing them away. The same goes for the conversation we have with ourselves. **'How can I value my worth?'** is much more powerful than **'What's wrong with me?'**

Even when we're aware of this, we may start off thinking about what we would like, and then very easily slip right back into thinking about what we don't want!

Amanda had the same problem. Every time she started thinking about what she wanted to say to people, she ended up feeling angry and not getting anywhere. This negative way of thinking is just a bad habit. For this reason, it's extremely useful to write down the positives of what we do want. It makes it clearer for us and it keeps us focused on connection and love and our own worthiness. Completing the *Don't Want – Do Want* worksheet was a big help in clarifying Amanda's needs, and asking for them to be met. She kindly agreed to share her worksheet as an example and I've included a blank version for you to download from the website.

Amanda's *Don't Want — Do Want* Worksheet

What is the DON'T WANT situation I want to change?	*My family and my friends not taking me for granted and treating me like dirt.*
In what ways is this DON'T WANT situation creating chaos in my life?	*I spend my life running from one thing to another, trying to keep everyone happy. I'm exhausted and I feel angry with them.*
I WOULD LIKE: If my life were calmer in this respect, what would that look like?	*I would like to be respected as a person.* *I would like people to respect my space.* *I would like people to acknowledge my feelings.*
I WOULD LIKE: What actions need to happen to get to this place of calm? (Remember to stay in the positive.)	*I would like people to remember that I'm available for phone calls only until 10 pm.* *I would like my family to communicate with each other when having a problem.* *I would like their help when I need it.*
What words / phrases do I need to use to make this clear? (To myself and to others)	*I care about myself.* *I'm worth it.* *I count.* *I will when I can.* *I'm important.* *My time is valuable.* *It's OK to say 'No' with kindness. It's saying 'Yes' to me!*

Completing the worksheet gave Amanda clarity and the confidence to make her boundaries clear to the people in her life and to ask for the worth and respect she deserved. And when she did so, nothing terrible happened, nobody abandoned her as she had feared — well, apart from the friend who hadn't invited her to her wedding, but Amanda now felt confident enough to let that friendship go!

As you fill out this worksheet you may notice that old familiar worries and physical sensations pop up for you. Perhaps you'll be having thoughts such as

'Yes but... What will they think... I can't say that...' and so forth.

Perhaps you'll be aware that your shoulders are tense, or your heart is pounding, or your stomach is churning. These are all reminders for you to tap a little more on letting go of your people-pleasing belief. So jot down the thoughts and any memories that come up and they'll be ready for your next tapping session.

Saying No with Kindness

When we're stressed, we tend to see things in black and white. It can seem as though we only have two choices: say 'Yes' to someone, or say 'No.' We may worry that saying 'No' means we're being unkind to them and pushing them away. However, saying 'No' is not being unkind if done with consideration and respect. It's useful to remember that when you say 'No' with consideration, you're also saying 'Yes' to yourself and thus connecting with your own worth.

If you're like many people, who find it difficult to say 'No,' here are some helpful tips.

Sandwiching a No

'Sandwiching a No' means you state your message in between a layer of kindness and a layer of affection for the other person. And when you focus on that *other* person's worth as well as your own, you're tuning each of you into the energy of worthiness, which can only ever be a good thing. Here's how the sandwich works:

First Layer: Start by truly acknowledging that person and letting them know you're paying attention to them. If it's appropriate, acknowledge something about them that you hold in regard.

Second Layer: Using the words you wrote on your *Don't Want — Do Want* worksheet, give them your message. Say 'No' clearly, but calmly. Remembering that when you say 'No,' you're saying 'Yes' to you.

Third Layer: When you've said 'No' firmly and made yourself clear, remind that person of something that you look forward to doing with them or that you wish them well.

Don't worry if this way of communicating feels awkward at first. As you practice it, it will become easier and flow more naturally.

Time Boundaries

The majority of us want to be good, kind, and caring. But in our bid to do so the word 'Yes' may tumble out of our mouths automatically when someone asks something of us. Later, we may well regret it and feel resentful because our own needs have been put aside, yet again.

Another great way to practice saying 'No' with kindness is to say 'Yes,' but from within your own time frame. This is helpful in letting go of a sense of constant obligation to others, whilst still being the kind and caring person you want to be.

For example:

'I'd love to help, but I'm busy right now — I do have a couple of hours on Thursday.'

When we try to resist those aspects of ourselves we don't like,

we actually give them more power, and so they continue to

exist in our lives.

Chapter Twelve
Into Love: The Power in Self-Acceptance

'When you're at peace with yourself and you love yourself, it's virtually impossible for you to do things to yourself that are destructive.'

Dr Wayne W. Dyer

'That's the fifth time you've said "I should" in the past ten minutes,' I gently challenged Theo. Often using words like 'I should' or 'I must,' is a sign that we're putting too much pressure on ourselves. It's as though we believe we're not enough and so we 'should' strive to be more.

Each time we talk to ourselves in these harsh ways, we place yet another block on the pathway to love. And yet, once we start to accept ourselves instead of criticising ourselves, we begin to clear that path. We begin to make room for love to flow back into our lives and provide us with the creativity and inspiration we need to make life easier again.

Practising self-acceptance always makes our relationships much better because there's no need to chase after approval: if we feel confident and at ease with ourselves we'll automatically do so with others. Self-acceptance then is a magical key to a happier life — something which many people don't realise, because they're so used to beating themselves up and always trying to prove themselves.

Remembering Self-acceptance

No Longer a Need To Prove

Connectedness
Creativity
Wisdom
Happiness

Allowing Creative Solutions

Better Relationships

Theo
Discovering True Success

The world of work very often requires creative solutions to problems. In our sessions, Theo realised that, rather than helping him, his constant need to prove himself had placed blocks in the flow of his creativity— it had been sabotaging his success. Looking back, he could clearly see how this need to prove had begun: his brother Frank's behaviour, and his parents' reactions to that, had always left him feeling left out, unnoticed, and not enough.

In his EFT practice, Theo was able to let go of the intensity of these experiences so that his belief about having to prove himself was no longer impacting on his life and the choices he made. This was a great help for Theo. He realised that letting go of the need to prove could only bring him success. He announced in one session:

'You know what, I've never really thought about it before, but I haven't really recognised me for me; I haven't loved myself or just accepted myself in the heart of me.'

And as he said this, he placed a hand on his chest and smiled, and my heart smiled too as I recognised that familiar loving energy in the room.

Self-Acceptance Empowers Us

If life has always been a struggle, learning to accept ourselves 'just as we are' can seem like a strange concept. Added to this, society in general is often focused on achievements and status: school, college, career, material wealth. Of course there's nothing wrong with wanting to do well in life. However, these ideas about success can make us confused about what self-acceptance really means. It's easy to get muddled up and think that self-acceptance means being lazy or giving in — when really it's a very important part of creating a successful life.

Self-acceptance empowers us, whilst pushing and trying to prove ourselves as 'good enough' inevitably sabotages our chances of success because it disempowers us by stripping away our confidence and stifling our creativity.

Carl Jung, the psychologist and founder of analytical psychology, made a very wise point:

'What you resist persists.'

When we try to resist those aspects of ourselves we don't like, we actually give them more power, and so they continue to exist in our lives. If we say to ourselves **'I'm no good,' 'I'm wrong,' 'I should do better,'** we're just making those negative ideas about ourselves seem bigger and more powerful, and therefore our sense of who we are seems smaller. If we choose not to pay those ideas too much attention, they become less potent. They don't get in the way of our success. When we can get clear on that, self-acceptance is much easier to recognise as a positive thing, because it matches with our desire to achieve and make a successful life.

And we've already seen how self-acceptance comes into the EFT practice. The set-up statement at the beginning always starts with an acknowledgement of a problem followed by some statement of acceptance such as:

'Even though I have this... I deeply love and accept myself.'

We do this to acknowledge where we're starting from and that we accept this problem as something that is only present in our lives at a particular moment in time; it's not more powerful or bigger than we are. It's just there and therefore we have the ability to let it go.

I'm going to share some practices in self-acceptance that have helped many people change their lives for the better. Before we go on to those practices, however, I just can't resist sharing with you a lovely example of how the power of love through acceptance helps build confidence and success.

Danny the Listening Dog

Today, there are children who are learning to improve their reading skills through the acceptance and love of a greyhound rescue dog, Danny.

Danny, with his owner Tony Nevett, visits primary schools and libraries all around the UK, making a huge difference to the lives of children through the Kennel Club 'Bark & Read' programme. As the children read out loud, it is Danny who listens to them; it's Danny who gives them a wag of the tail and a lick; and those children, some of them shy and lacking in confidence, are able to improve their behaviour, their concentration, and their reading skills.

What is Danny the dog doing for those children? He's helping them to let go of any fear of being judged, any need to prove themselves as good enough, and by the power of love through simply accepting them, he gives them space to be able to learn to read and grow confident. You can find out more about the Bark and Read scheme in 'Resources.'

Three Practices in Self-Acceptance

The Permitting Thoughts Exercise

We've already seen the impact of thoughts in some of the previous exercises. Our thoughts dictate all our experiences. What we think about a situation can make the difference between it being a problem or a challenge, or a negative or a positive. It's very helpful then to observe the thoughts we're thinking on a daily basis and notice how many of them are self-judging and self-critical.

In my experience, people are often alarmed when they realise just how much they've been mentally beating themselves up! If this is you, don't worry. Every single person who starts noticing their thinking patterns goes through this stage of dismay at the amount of negative self-talk that's going on! Noticing it is a normal part of the process; the trick is to avoid beating yourself up about this too! So just give yourself permission to have had the negative thoughts you've had and follow this up with:

> **'Ok, I've had that thought; it's not so helpful for me ... so what other thoughts can I use to be kinder and more accepting of myself?'**

That's all any of us need do — give ourselves permission to be human first. Then seek out kinder thoughts. It's surprising how quickly we can begin to move into self-acceptance by first accepting that negative thoughts are just a natural part of life, and then letting them go instead of battling against them. I've lost count of the number of people who've told me how good it feels to finally give themselves permission to love themselves just as they are, even when they're grumpy!

The *Tweaking Thoughts* Exercise

Accepting that you have negative thoughts is the very first point of change. The *Tweaking Thoughts* exercise is the next step towards feeling much, much happier.

It's about catching your self-critical thoughts, accepting them, but then tweaking them into kinder and more accepting ways to talk to yourself.

To begin, draw a table with two columns. In the left-hand column, write down a self-critical thought that you've noticed. For example:

> **'I always put my foot in it!'**

Self-Critical Thought	More Accepting Thought
I always put my foot in it.	

In the right-hand column, put in a more accepting thought.

But be careful. An important part of this exercise is *not* to try and put in an *opposite* thought. For example:

'I never put my foot in it; I am the soul of discretion!'

If you try to put in a completely opposite thought, your mind will argue back.

... 'Who are you trying to kid?'

So an example of tweaking to a more accepting thought in this case would be:

'Yes, I've been known to put my foot in it — we all do that occasionally. I also have times when I'm aware and considerate of others.'

I've included some further examples for you in the table below.

Each time you write in a more accepting thought in the right-hand column, draw a line through the self-critical thought you've written in the left-hand column. This gives your mind a very powerful message that you want to change the established unhelpful thinking pattern that has been your habit.

Self-Critical Thought	More Accepting Thought
~~I always put my foot in it.~~	*Yes, I have been known to put my foot in it — we all do that occasionally. I also have times when I'm aware and considerate of others.*
~~I'm a failure!~~	*There was that time when I achieved...* *And that other time when I...*
~~I'll never change.~~	*I'm filling out this exercise, so I'm obviously having a go at making changes.*
~~I should have fixed this by now.~~	*Maybe it would have been helpful to work on it before. But I was thinking differently then. It's great that I'm making a start now and I can continue to do so step by step.*

Complete this exercise each day for at least a week and you'll find your negative self-talk diminishes.

My Life on a Good Enough Day

This next exercise, like many of the exercises in this book, is simple yet powerfully transformative. It's about imagining what a 'good enough day' in your life would be like and writing that down. Many people have found this exercise helps in making a shift from the heavy weight of constant self-disapproval to the lightness of self-acceptance. Here are some tips for writing it:

» Start it in the present tense — *Today I am...*

» Try to write at least one page.

» Write as many more pages as you like.

» Try not to get too bogged down in what you won't be doing, i.e. *I won't moan and judge myself.* Instead, focus more on the positive statements such as *I will say kind and accepting things to myself.*

» Mention the words 'good enough' on several occasions.

» End on a loving note.

Theo kindly agreed to share the piece he wrote for this exercise.

My Life on a Good Enough Day

Today I wake up and the first thing that comes into my mind is appreciation. I turn over in bed and I see my wife there, still asleep, and I feel lucky for all the good things in my life. I don't worry about all the things I have to do in the future and all the things I've got wrong in the past. Today is good enough as it is: no worries about time, or money, or wishing I was more or could make more. I'm just going to be who I am, as I am, at least for today.

I know that today, I'm good enough for my wife and for my sons, too. I'm so proud of my family and I'll tell them that again today, and when they tell me the same, I will truly listen to them and say 'Thank you,' instead of batting away their compliments as I usually do.

Today, I'm going to the business training centre. I'm going to start my course on running a small business. It seems crazy now that I haven't asked for this sort of help before because I thought it would make me look inadequate. All that struggling for no reason! But I'm not going to judge myself for that; I thought differently then and today I'm just going to go along and see how they can help. It can't do any harm, and whatever advice they give me can only be a good thing. I'm not going to worry about impressing the trainers on the course: I have nothing to prove — after all they are there to teach me, so I'm going to go in with an open heart and put my trust in them.

Today, as it's my special 'Good Enough Day,' I'll listen out for that voice in my head which says 'You Must' and 'You Should' — the one that tells me I'm not as clever or as special as other people and that I must try harder. I know this is the voice of who I was a long time ago when I was just a lonely, unloved boy. So when I hear that voice I won't be cross with it, I'll just say to that little boy within me that it's OK, it's all OK, and he is plenty good enough.

As I write this letter, it occurs to me that I must be doing something right to have my wife still by my side after all these years.

I don't have to prove myself as special to her, I am OK and I am loved. I am OK today because it is a Good Enough Day.

Completing this exercise, or simply reading through the example here, can be a moving experience because it can bring up such a sense of release. If you feel heart-warmed by it, or tearful, or any other feeling at all, that's OK. You're good enough as you are in the present moment, however that may be.

It's often the case that all these good, supportive people have been there all the time, but we've been so blinkered by trying to prove we can stand alone that we haven't been able to connect with them.

Chapter Thirteen
Into Love: The Power in Trust

'So herein lies the simple solution. It really is simple. Here it is.
Go out and connect with people. And connect as yourself!'
Dr David Hamilton

People sometimes make the mistake of thinking that doing every-thing by themselves means they'll feel stronger and more confident. Certainly we all need to be independent to a certain degree. However, there's a big difference between having inner confidence and being so overly independent that we fear asking for help in case it makes us look weak or stupid. Truly confident people feel secure enough to ask for support when they need it and they trust it will be forthcoming.

Think about very successful people; they all have a support team behind them who they trust to share the load. When we put our trust in others and share our needs with them, we feel supported and confident that we're not alone. In turn, this gives us space to grow as people because we're not spending all our time and energy struggling alone.

David
Trust in Connection

David realised that his constant need to prove his independence was the cause of his panic attacks. No one at his job at the bank was putting pressure on him. He was doing that all by himself; the more stressed he became, the more he felt he should keep his worries to himself. That's just how his life had always been. He didn't tell anyone at work that he was struggling because he didn't want to look like he couldn't cope, and because he didn't know who he could trust to talk to. But squashing down his fear wasn't helping because it just made itself apparent through his anxiety attacks.

Looking back, David recognised that his need to be so overly independent had started in his childhood due to his family's disapproval whenever he showed any feelings of vulnerability or dependency. He recalled a number of experiences that had led him to believe that he should never ask for help or support from anyone. EFT practice was a big help to David in clearing the emotional impact of these experiences and letting go of this unhelpful way of approaching life. Now it was time to learn to trust in the support of others — something that his need to go it alone had deprived him of all his life.

Actually, David had already made this first step in trusting when he sought out my help through therapy. Though when I asked him how he felt about coming to see me, he said:

> **'I feel like a failure, having to come and get help — I should be able to deal with this by myself. What if I've come here for help and I still don't get better?'**

It made me sad to think that this young man was struggling through life thinking that he couldn't or shouldn't trust in the support of others. But I was also impressed that he'd made the brave move to seek help. No doubt the intensity of his anxiety attacks had forced him to reach out for help. However, from my many years of helping people transform their lives, I knew that, at some deeply profound level, life was nudging David to take a step on his journey into wisdom— and this was going to be a big step.

Before long, David began to trust in the connection we were establishing in the therapy room, and in time he began to take that trust and test it out with other people. He came into one session and announced his astonishment: he'd told one of his colleagues about his panic attacks and his colleague had shared that he'd had exactly the same thing! This was life-changing for David as he began to acknowledge that he could share his fears on an intimate level with other people; other people wouldn't laugh at him or scorn him for being weak. David's confidence increased tenfold as he opened up to the idea of sharing with others.

Knowing Who to Trust

When people seek help in therapy, they expect that their therapist will have the skills in place and the emotional capacity to help them. But what about being able to trust that other people will be willing and able to offer help? That may feel risky, especially if you haven't been used to sharing your feelings and worries.

It's possible that some people may be feeling overwhelmed by their own problems and so they they're not in a good place to listen and help you. So how can you know who to trust? There is a way to know this.

Think about happy people— they're content and secure in life because of their ability to share their feelings and support each other. And very importantly, they're able to identify who's likely to be supportive because they're already *in the zone*; they're already tuned in to the power of love because they treat themselves accordingly. As we've seen in the last three chapters, when we treat ourselves with kindness, worthiness, and acceptance, we tune in to love and we attract these ways of being into our lives. The kinder we are to ourselves, the more we'll attract kindness from others; the more we have regard for our own worth, the more we'll attract this same worth from others;

the more we accept ourselves, the more acceptance we'll attract from others.

It's often the case that all these good, supportive people have been there all the time, but we've been so blinkered by trying to prove we can stand alone that we haven't been able to connect with them. Once we start treating ourselves in these new ways, we open the door to the magical support of love, which reorganises everything in our favour so that the right people are there for us, and now our eyes are opened so that we can recognise them!

Observing the Miracles Happening Every Day

Each part of The Transformation Process is about trust, about letting go of fear, and learning to have faith in the magical power of love. In Part One we reassured the little child within; in Part Two we began relinquishing those beliefs about struggle; and in Part Three we've been looking at the practices of self-kindness, self-worth, and self-acceptance to help connect with the support that love always brings. What better way to add to these practices, than to remind ourselves that we can trust in the power of love through observing the miracles happening every around us?

This magical power makes itself known in every blade of grass, every drop of rain, every flight of a bird—everywhere in nature. When we were children, nature showed us that we were part of something grand and giving, something that we could trust to sustain all life, without question. As adults we can get back to that sense of trust by going into nature. It's a good way to experience the energy of connectedness again, and in doing so we can begin to trust that we can indeed have connectedness with others too.

Three Practices in Trust

Grounding in Nature

Recent research (see 'Resources' for details) tells us that we can actually change how we feel by how we use our body. Our posture, our breathing, our facial expressions, how we walk—all these can be arranged to instil a great sense of confidence and trust. Combining a practice in posture with being out in nature brings a great sense of focus and calm. Here's how it works. Whenever you're out in nature, place your attention on the ground beneath your feet. If you can walk barefoot, all the better, but if not, you can still benefit from this exercise if you are wearing shoes. Become aware of the points below your big toes, your little toes, and your heels, make sure you feel an even pressure on these points and really connect them with the ground beneath you.

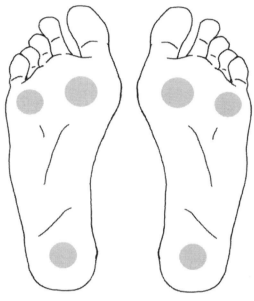

As you centre yourself in this way, become aware that you're connecting in with the power of the entire universe; feel the inner strength that comes from that energy flowing through you, holding you safe, loving you. Breathe deeply from the core of your body and know that you are at one with our universe.

Five-Point Body Language Checklist

I've already mentioned that those people who practise self-kindness, self-worth, and self-acceptance are very likely going to be open and supportive to others. This is often noticeable in the way they speak and their body language. As I said in Chapter Two: 'Why Is My Life Such a Struggle,' much of the way we communicate is indirect and subtle. A lot of the time we're giving off signals without even realising we're doing so. You can gauge a lot about another person's willingness to be open and supportive to you by observing their body language. Body language is a wide topic and many books have written on the subject (see 'Resources'). If you find it hard to decide if a person is likely to be supportive in your times of need, it's useful to have a handy checklist to observe their body language. Here's a five-point list. People who are in a good emotional space to offer you support will:

» Tend to make clear space between you and themselves, no folded arms, legs or objects placed between you

» Hold a steady gaze, maintain eye contact, and keep their head fairly still

» Repeat back the emotional words you've used: you're angry, happy etc.

» Tilt their head or body towards you when you speak

» Mirror your actions, such as picking up a glass at the same time

Trust through Guided Visualisation

Another great way to create trust in a relationship and connecting is through guided meditation. I've created a guided meditation especially for you called *Trust.mp3*. You can download this at the website:

And then life becomes an adventure; fear is gone. Now the power of love is running the show! I see this time and again, and it always makes my heart sing and my soul smile.

Chapter Fourteen
An Ongoing Journey

'"I wonder," he said, "whether the stars are set alight in heaven so that one day each one of us may find his own again..."'
Antoine de Saint-Exupéry

D ear Reader, it has been wonderful to share with you throughout this journey. As we come towards the end of our time together, let's look back at the path we've travelled.

We started by looking at something I've discovered from many years of helping people: that true happiness comes from living in harmony with the metaphysical elements of life itself: creativity, connectedness, and evolving into wisdom. Once we have these in place, we're able to approach our relationships, our work — every adventure and every challenge — supported, confident, and inspired.

We've seen that living this way is natural to us in our early childhood when we feel connected with the intelligent and loving power that sustains all life. However, that connection soon gets lost through the misguided messages we receive as we're growing up. Those messages about being separate from love and having to earn approval and acceptance are messages based in fear. They lead us to form limiting beliefs that shape the lens through which we view life from that point on. We've seen how these limiting beliefs create struggle in our adult life; they get in the way of our ability to connect well in our relationships (with self and others), and they get in the way of our creativity and our ability to grow and become wiser. We've seen how these beliefs can be difficult to shift for two reasons: because they reside in the subconscious and because the little child we once were is still there struggling away, running the show. This makes it hard to love ourselves — even when we know that love is the answer.

To help you move out of fear and back into love, I've shared The Transformation Process: a specific method of emotional healing developed through my work over thousands of client sessions. I've taken you through this process: first reassuring the little child within that they can let go of their need to struggle, then working to clear those beliefs from the subconscious with the remarkable and powerful EFT technique. Finally, we focused on bringing back self-love, and in particular self-kindness, self-worth, self-acceptance, and trust — those self-loving ways of being that limiting beliefs about struggle make us forget.

Before we say goodbye, let me update you on the four clients who kindly agreed to share their stories with us. Of course you'll have guessed that I changed their names for confidentiality, and in the true spirit of this book, I gave them names that are all connected with the power of love in some form.

'Grace' means kindness and love towards mankind.

'Amanda' means worthy of being loved.

'Theo' means God-given.

'David' means beloved.

Grace

Grace practiced EFT every morning. She was surprised at how rapidly all those distressing childhood memories cleared — of course she could still remember events, but the emotional intensity attached to those memories had diminished to the point that they no longer impacted on her life. Her need to go through life 'Being Strong' faded away and she was learning to be kinder to herself every day. By living from this new perspective, Grace's life became less of a hardship; she realised she could make a life of her own choosing, rather than feeling she had to put up with whatever 'just happened' to her. As her hardships disappeared, so did her need to soothe herself with addictive behaviours. She began to attract kind and supportive friends into her life, and she began to see inspiring opportunities for her future. She said:

'It's an interesting thing, this being kind to myself — it makes me feel strong inside, like I have choices. I can choose what makes me happy instead of trying to keep coping with what doesn't!'

Amanda

When Amanda began her EFT practice, her long-held belief that she had to keep pleasing people simply disappeared. She took a very different perspective on life. She became much more assertive with her family and friends. This was a big step in Amanda's journey into wisdom as she began to recognise that she'd always deserved respect — she'd just been looking in all the wrong places for it. Not surprisingly, her sense of confidence soared as she started putting appropriate boundaries into place and re-claimed her self-worth.

Amanda was surprised at how quickly her friends and family changed towards her. They didn't abandon her, as she'd feared they would. Instead they were much more courteous and respectful towards to her. Her friends began to include her in their social gatherings and helped her out when she asked. When Amanda wasn't there to play go-between anymore, her family members actually began to get on much better with each other, and she started to enjoy their company more. Amanda told me in our last session:

'I actually really like my family now. I feel closer with them — all that having to keep them happy and me resenting it was getting in the way. I feel much happier when I'm around them now.'

Theo

In our last session, Theo said,

'I feel like I'm me, but a better me!'

I smiled at the man who'd once told me that he was sick of struggling with life and didn't think he could ever be happy. He practiced EFT each day, tapping on the memories from his childhood that had led him to believe proving himself was the only way to get through life. As he did this, he began to think in a completely different way; he recognised that his old way of struggling to gain approval could never bring him real happiness. The exercise *My Life on a Good Enough Day* had a profound effect on Theo; it helped him find self-acceptance which brought him peace, inner courage, and a sense of creative enthusiasm for life ahead.

When he told me that he finally felt like he was making a success of his life, I wondered if the old 'I need to prove myself' was still there to some degree. But when I queried him about that, he smiled and shook his head.

'Now I see that a successful life isn't about proving that I'm good enough — I am good enough! I'm already a success: my family and all that I do is just fine. I feel like a huge weight has left me.'

David

At our last session, David was in a rush to leave on time. It was February 14th and he had a special date with his girlfriend. He hadn't had a panic attack in a good while and I was so pleased for him. He grinned,

'You know what? I know Valentine's is for romance, but today I really feel like I love MYSELF!'

David had fully embraced his EFT practice and was tapping each day as part of his morning routine. Each time, he cleared more of the emotional impact of long-ago experiences that had led him to believe he had to do everything by himself. David was now much more relaxed and able to relate with his work colleagues without fear of being judged.

Alongside his EFT practice, David had taken up meditation. He said it made him feel confident and that there was something bigger to life: his problems seemed small — just things to think about, ways to learn about life.

I was happy for David. Our sessions had been hard work for him at first because he'd found it hard to trust and share his feelings with me. Now he was a relaxed, confident, young man: panic-free, with a happy life ahead of him.

A Beautiful Phenomenon

Through The Transformation Process, I've seen so many people change their lives as they move out of fear and into love. And each time I'm lucky to be witness to a beautiful phenomenon. Once people begin to let go of their need to struggle, they begin to see their life through a very different lens. They awaken their creative energy and understand that they can be masters of their own destiny. They begin to connect well; they begin to have a great relationship — with themselves, with others, with life itself. They no longer have problems that keep them stuck, rather they embrace each challenge as an opportunity to figure out how to grow and become wiser. And then life becomes an adventure — fear is gone. Now the power of love is running the show! I see this time and again, and it always makes my heart sing and my soul smile when people say things like:

'You know what? I want to change my work and do something more meaningful… I've fallen in love with life… I've just begun to see that actually I can do anything I want.'

When people say things like this, it tells me that their little child within has let go of the need to protect them and is feeling enthusiastic and free again. It shows me that life is no longer a path of endless obstacles to overcome, but has become a path of ease with interesting and inspiring challenges. This is the life that every one of us can have. There's nothing to prove and no reason to feel that we have to struggle and worry all the time.

An Extraordinary Adventure

Whatever dreams and desires each of us holds, however we want to create the story of our life, the magic of love will always be there waiting to guide and support us because, contrary to what we've thought, love can *never* run out.

And how will you go on to create your own story now?

Of course, leading a life of true happiness doesn't mean that you'll never fall out with another person, get irritated, make mistakes at work, or have frustrations. Life is filled with these challenges each and every day — this is what it's all about.

But if you continue with the practices you've learnt in this book, your life is going to be an extraordinary adventure—an exciting, ongoing journey into wisdom.

So remember to practice EFT every day. Make tapping a part of your routine, just like brushing your teeth: that way, you'll find it easier to keep up the practice. Keep a journal of your thoughts and write down memories of events that you'd like to tap on. Note down questions about the challenges in your life too, and as you make this a habit, you'll find that what once seemed tangled becomes clear. Remember to stay friends with the little child within, reassuring them of how worthy they are. Continue on with your self-love practices and always remember that a little bit of self-loving, such as a kind act to yourself, an accepting thought, recognising support in the heart of another, goes a long way. And as you travel this ongoing journey into love and wisdom, you'll find that hanging around for long in any state of unhappiness will be less tolerable, and that the old, struggling ways of viewing the world will no longer feel right for you.

Your Greatest Ever Wisdom Step

Moving 'Out Of Fear and Into Love' is the greatest wisdom step you can ever take. It's the biggest of the big adventures, the most important of the wise lessons, and the grandest of your grand achievements.

Dear Reader: it's time to say goodbye for now. It's been an honour and a privilege to share this time with you. I wish for you so much happiness, so much wisdom, and so much love in your life.

Until we connect again…

With Love

Marléne Rose Shaw

Don't forget, you can find all your bonuses at the website.

If you liked this book, it would be a great help if you would add a review on Amazon. In this way, you can send love forward and share the benefits of it with others. Thank you!

You can also add your email address so that I can let you know when I have further books, downloads and useful resources for you.

References

Chapter 1: The Universal Elements of Happiness

Dyer, Dr Wayne D, PhD., *The Power of Intention,* Hay House, 2004

Chapter 2: Why is My Life Such a Struggle?

Jeffers, Susan, *End The Struggle and Dance With Life,* Hodder Paperbacks; New Ed edition, 2005

Nin, Anaïs, The Quotable Anaïs Nin: 365 Quotations with Citations, Sky Blue Press; 1st edition, 2015

Chapter 3: How We Learnt To Struggle

Hay, Louise, *You Can Heal Your Life,* Hay House, 1984

Chapter 4: Why It's So Hard to Change

Lipton, Bruce H., The Biology of Belief: Unleashing the Power of Consciousness, Matter & Miracles, Hay House, 2011

Chapter 5: Introducing The Transformation Process

Dyer, Dr Wayne D, PhD., www.revolutionalminds.com/wayne-dyer-quotes 2015

Chapter 6: A Very Important Friendship

Coelho, Paulo, *The Alchemist,* Harper Collins, 1993

Chapter 7: Clearing Away the Fear Clutter

Schuman, Helen, *Course in Miracles,* Foundation for Inner Peace, 3rd edition, 2008

Chapter 8: Practicing Emotional Freedom Techniques

Craig, Gary, The Eft Manual (Everyday Eft: Emotional Freedom Techniques), Elite Books, 2011

Craig, Gary, www.emofree.com

Chapter 9: Into Love – The Power

Planck, Max, As quoted in Braden, Gregg, *The Spontaneous Healing of Belief*, Hay House, 2012

McTaggart, Lynne, *The Field: The Quest for the Secret Force of the Universe*, Element, 2003

Chapter 10: Into Love – The Power in Self-Kindness

Coenn, Daniel, Niccolo Machiavelli: His Words xxx ??? 2014

Hamilton, David R., PhD., Why Kindness is Good For You, Hay House, 2010

Chapter 11: Into Love – The Power in Self-Worth

Hay, Louise, *Adventures of Lulu,* Hay House, 2005

Chapter 12: Into Love – The Power in Self-Acceptance

Dyer, Dr Wayne D., Ph.D, *Staying On The Path* Audio CD, Hay House, 2006

Chapter 13: Into Love – The Power in Trust

Hamilton David R., PhD., *I Heart Me: The Science Of Self-Love* Hay House, 2015

Chapter 14: An Ongoing Journey

Saint-Exupéry, Antoine de and Woods, Katherine, *The Little Prince*, Egmont, 2001

Resources

Books

Dispenza, Joe, D.C *Breaking the Habit of Being Yourself*, Hay House, 2012

Fry, Wendy, *Find You Find Love: Get to the heart of love and relationships using EFT*, Be Positive, 2014

Teversham, Liesel, *No Problem: The Upside of Saying No*, Kima Global Publishers, 2013

The Kennel Club "Bark & Read" Programme, www.thekennelclub. org.uk/our-resources/bark-and-read/

Dyer, Dr. Wayne D, PhD., *The Power of Intention*, Hay House, 2004

Erikson, Milton, *Creative Choice in Hypnosis: The Seminars, Workshops and Lectures of Milton H. Erickson*, Free Association Books, 1998

Craig, Gary *The EFT Manual*, Elite Books, 2011

Braden, Gregg, *The Divine Matrix: Bridging Time, Space, Miracles, and Belief*, Hay House, 2008

Hamilton, David R., PhD., *I Heart Me: The Science Of Self-Love* Hay House, 2015

Websites

Founder of EFT, Gary Craig www.emofree.com

Hay House www.hayhouse.co.uk

Marléne Rose Shaw wwwmarleneroseshaw.com

About The Author

Marléne Rose Shaw, BA (Hons) App. Psych is a therapist and an EFT and Matrix Reimprinting Practitioner. She has a thriving practice in the UK and online.

Over the past twenty years she's helped thousands of people change their lives for the better. She is passionate about helping people overcome problems that have been keeping them stuck and unhappy, to move forward to become the creators of their own lives and destinies.

Contact Details:

For one-to-one sessions via Skype or at my practice:

www.marleneroseshaw.com

info@marleneroseshaw.com

Facebook: www.facebook.com/outoffearintolove

Twitter: twitter.com/MarleneRoseShaw